**30% HAPPIER
IN 30 DAYS**

30% HAPPIER IN 30 DAYS

A QUICK START TO A HAPPIER, HEALTHIER YOU

DANIEL G. AMEN, MD

#1 *NEW YORK TIMES* BESTSELLING AUTHOR

TYNDALE
REFRESH™

Think Well. Live Well. Be Well.

Visit Tyndale online at tyndale.com.

Tyndale and Tyndale's quill logo are registered trademarks of Tyndale House Ministries. *Tyndale Refresh* and the Tyndale Refresh logo are trademarks of Tyndale House Ministries. Tyndale Refresh is a nonfiction imprint of Tyndale House Publishers, Carol Stream, Illinois.

30% Happier in 30 Days: A Quick Start to a Happier, Healthier You

Adapted from *You, Happier*, published in 2022 under ISBN 978-1-4964-5452-2

Designed by Sarah Susan Richardson

Published in association with the literary agency of WordServe Literary Group, www.wordserveliterary.com.

For information about special discounts for bulk purchases, please contact Tyndale House Publishers at csresponse@tyndale.com, or call 1-855-277-9400.

Library of Congress Cataloging-in-Publication Data

A catalog record for this book is available from the Library of Congress.

ISBN 978-1-4964-7234-2

Printed in the United States of America

29	28	27	26	25	24	23
7	6	5	4	3	2	1

Contents

Introduction: The Seven Secrets to Happiness No One Is Talking About *1*

Day 1 Your Brain on Happiness *11*

Day 2 Know Your Brain Type *16*

Day 3 11 Essential Strategies to Optimize Your Brain *23*

Day 4 Natural Ways to Feel Good *32*

Day 5 Happy Foods vs. Sad Foods *36*

Day 6 Controlling Your Negative Thoughts *44*

Day 7 Focus on Behaviors You Like *48*

Day 8 Micro-Moments of Happiness *52*

Day 9 At the Core of Your Happiness *57*

Day 10 Know Your Purpose in Six Questions *60*

Day 11 Tame Your Inner Dragons *65*

Day 12 A Little TLC Goes a Long Way *70*

Day 13 Don't Let ANTs Ruin Your Picnic *74*

Day 14 Laughter Is the Best Medicine *79*

Day 15 Good Nights = Happier Days *84*

Day 16 Where Your Mind Goes,
         Your Mood Follows *87*

Day 17 Create Your Own Safe Haven *92*

Day 18 Look for the Positive *95*

Day 19 Practice Loving-Kindness *100*

Day 20 The Power of Gratitude *103*

Day 21 Live in the Moment *106*

Day 22 Accentuate the Positive *111*

Day 23 Eliminate the Negative *115*

Day 24 Just Breathe *123*

Day 25 It's All Relative *128*

Day 26 Don't Worry, Be Hygge *146*

Day 27 Get Happy the Nor Way! *152*

Day 28 That's the Spirit! *156*

Day 29 Love—Your Secret Weapon *161*

Day 30 The Most Important Question to
         Ask Yourself *166*

About the Author *171*

Notes *177*

THE SEVEN SECRETS TO HAPPINESS NO ONE IS TALKING ABOUT

"Thirty days ago I was so miserable, so hopeless, and so depressed! This has literally transformed my life and made my life not only bearable but JOYFUL."

30-DAY HAPPINESS CHALLENGE PARTICIPANT

CONTRARY TO WHAT MOST people believe, happiness is not reserved for the rich, famous, fortunate, or beautiful. As a psychiatrist, I've treated many of these people, and they are some of the unhappiest people I know. You don't have to win the genetic lottery to be blessed with a happy disposition, and you aren't doomed to always feel down when life doesn't go your way.

For decades, social scientists have been searching for the roots of happiness. Based on their research, it is generally accepted that happiness is about 40 percent genetic, 10 percent your situation in life or what happens to you, and 50 percent habits and mindset. This means you have a higher degree of control over happiness than most people think.

In 2021, in the wake of the pandemic, I launched an online 30-Day Happiness Challenge that attracted an astounding 32,000 participants. I asked them to take the Oxford Happiness Questionnaire, a well-respected assessment that provides a score on a scale of 1 to 6.[1] (You can take the quiz at www.amen university.com/oxford.)

On each day of the challenge, I shared science-backed tips and strategies that ramp up happiness and positivity. I wanted to see how much the participants could improve over the course of the challenge, so people took the quiz twice, once at the beginning of the program and once at the end. The average happiness score for participants on day 1 was 3.58, which correlates to being "not particularly happy." Among people who completed the course, the average score on day 30 had jumped to 4.36, a 22 percent improvement, which correlates with being "rather happy; pretty happy"! Even more impressive, their self-reported happiness levels increased by 32 percent. And they did it in just about 10 to 15 minutes a day. This shows that not only can you develop happiness, but also that you can do it quickly.

Why should we focus on being happy? Extensive research has shown that happiness is associated with a lower heart rate, lower blood pressure, and overall heart health. Happier people get fewer infections, have lower cortisol levels (the hormone of stress), and have fewer aches and pains. Happy people tend to live longer, have better relationships, and be more successful in their careers. Plus happiness is contagious because happier people tend to make others happier.[2]

Researchers typically report happiness being associated with novelty, fun experiences, positive relationships, laughter, gratitude, anticipation, helping others, staying away from comparisons, meditation, nature, living in the moment (rather than the past with regret or the future with fear), productive work, a sense of purpose, spiritual beliefs, and wanting what you have as opposed to wanting more. Yet most happiness research completely misses seven important aspects. I call them the seven secrets to happiness that no one is talking about.

Secret 1: Know your brain type. Taking a one-size-fits-all approach to people with any mental health issue based solely on their symptoms invites failure and frustration. In 1991, I started looking at the brain with SPECT (single photon emission computed tomography) imaging. SPECT looks at how the brain functions and basically tells us three things about brain activity: if it is healthy, underactive, or overactive.

- If the brain showed full, even, symmetrical activity overall, we called it **Balanced**.

- If the front part of the brain was sleepy or lower in activity compared to others, the person was more likely to be creative, impulsive, and **Spontaneous**.

- If the front part of the brain was much more active than average, the person tended to worry and be more **Persistent**.

- If the emotional or limbic brain was more active than average, the person tended to be more vulnerable to sadness and be more **Sensitive.**

- If the amygdala and basal ganglia were more active than average, the person tended to be more anxious and **Cautious.**

Understanding your type of brain is critical to understanding who you are, how you think, how you act, how you interact with other humans' brains, and what makes you happy.

Secret 2: Optimize the physical functioning of your brain. Your brain is the organ of happiness. With a healthy brain, you are happier (because you've made better decisions), healthier (also better decisions), wealthier (better decisions), and more successful in relationships, work, and everything else you do. The quality of your decisions (a brain function) is the common denominator of happiness and success in every area of life, so if you want to be happy, it is critical to assess and optimize the physical functioning of your brain.

Secret 3: Nourish your unique brain. New research suggests we can produce up to 700 new brain cells a day if we put them in a nourishing environment (meaning good nutrition, omega-3 fatty acids, oxygen, blood flow, and stimulation).[3] If we nourish our brain and body, the hippocampi can grow stronger. We have two hippocampi, one in our left temporal lobe and another in our right temporal lobe. They are critical for learning, memory, and mood (happiness). With a few basic nutrients and targeted supplements, you can improve the health of your brain and support the brain chemicals involved in your happiness.

Secret 4: Choose foods you love that love you back. It is becoming abundantly clear that if you want to feel good, you need to eat well. In a 2017 study, researchers found that when people with moderate to severe depression received nutritional counseling and ate a more healthful diet for 12 weeks, their symptoms improved significantly. In fact, depressive symptoms got so much better that over 32 percent of the participants no longer qualified as having a mood disorder.[4] Based on these results, the research team suggested that dietary changes could be an effective treatment strategy for depression.

Secret 5: Master your mind and gain psychological distance from the noise in your head. Your mind can be a troublemaker. Thoughts and feelings come from many sources, such as the news, music, social media, personal experiences, memories, genetic tendencies, and much, much more. The good news is you are *not* your mind. That is why your ability to separate from, manage, and not be a victim of your mind is essential to feeling happy.

Secret 6: Notice what you like about others more than what you don't. I know you've heard the phrase "It takes two to make a relationship better." That's just not my experience as a psychiatrist. When I teach my patients how powerful they are—how they can influence their loved one's behavior—they realize they have the power to make their relationships better or worse, and so can you!

Secret 7: Live each day based on your clearly defined values, purpose, and goals. Over the years, I've seen many patients who feel disconnected and insignificant. They lack a sense of meaning and purpose. They lack a relationship with God or something bigger than themselves. Having a deep sense of meaning and purpose gives you a reason to get up in the morning, and focusing on doing what you love to do is a sure-fire way to make you happier.

Now that you know the seven secrets of happiness, let's get serious about helping you become and stay happier. Let me begin by assuring you that none of what I have written about in this book is complicated or hard. That said, as you work through the program, you'll have good days and bad days, ups and downs. Don't let the down days discourage you. Learn from them so you can make better decisions in the future.

Nothing is more important to your health and happiness than the quality of the decisions you make, and consistently making high-quality decisions will give you a high-quality life. So post these seven secrets where you can see them every day. If your mood lags or unhappiness starts to creep into your mind, ask yourself what you can do to make it better.

You can do this! Just go to www.amenuniversity .com/oxford, take the assessment, and get ready to become a happier, healthier you!

YOUR BRAIN ON HAPPINESS

YOUR BRAIN IS THE ORGAN of happiness. Your brain is the organ of liking, wanting, and learning—all essential ingredients that go into happiness. Your brain is also the organ of sadness, anxiety, panic, anger, and storing past emotional trauma—the enemies of happiness. Deciding to assess and optimize the three pounds of tissue between your ears is the first foundational decision to a happier life. Yet most people never think about their brains, which is a huge mistake because success and happiness start in the physical functioning of the brain. But with a better brain comes a better, happier, and more successful life. That said, let's take a quick tour of your brain.

YOUR BRAIN: A QUICK TOUR

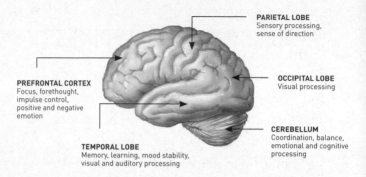

PARIETAL LOBE
Sensory processing,
sense of direction

OCCIPITAL LOBE
Visual processing

CEREBELLUM
Coordination, balance,
emotional and cognitive
processing

PREFRONTAL CORTEX
Focus, forethought,
impulse control,
positive and negative
emotion

TEMPORAL LOBE
Memory, learning, mood stability,
visual and auditory processing

Your brain houses a primitive section, responsible for the activities essential for survival. Neuroscientists call this the "reptilian brain," and it includes the brain stem and cerebellum, which control breathing, heart rate, body temperature, balance, and coordination. The brain stem and cerebellum play a critical role in happiness, as they are also involved in processing speed and producing some of the chemicals, such as dopamine and serotonin, that are involved in mood, motivation, and learning.

The human brain also has a limbic, or emotional, brain that is situated around the brain stem and cerebellum. This brain region colors our emotions as positive or negative and is involved with our basic needs for survival, including bonding, nesting, and emotions. The limbic brain records memories of what sustains or threatens our survival and is responsible for our urges and cravings (our wants and desires) and how pleasurable something is (our likes). The limbic brain exerts a strong, often unconscious, influence on our behavior.

Limbic brain structures include:

- **Hippocampus**: mood and the formation of new memories
- **Amygdala**: emotions, including fear, as well as signaling the presence of food, sexual partners, rivals, or children in distress
- **Hypothalamus**: helps control body temperature, appetite, sexual behavior, and emotions
- **Basal ganglia**: motivation, pleasure, smoothing motor movements
- **Anterior cingulate gyrus**: attention shifting and error detection

Finally, the brain has one other area known as the cerebral cortex. This part of the brain is involved in creating and understanding language, abstract thought, imagination, and culture. It has endless learning possibilities and creates the story of why we are happy or sad, which may or may not have anything to do with the truth.

Information from the world enters your brain through your senses and goes to the limbic brain, where it is tagged as meaningful, safe, or dangerous; then it travels to the back part of the brain (temporal, parietal, and occipital lobes), where it is initially processed and compared with past experience; then it travels to the front part of the brain for you to evaluate and decide if you will act on it. Information in the brain travels up to 270 miles per hour, and the transmission of information from the outside world to your conscious awareness happens almost instantaneously.

Happiness relies on quieting the misery-producing areas of the brain. In particular, this means calming activity in the amygdala, an area that registers fear, and the insular cortex, a region located between the frontal and temporal lobes that is more active when people feel angst or unhappiness.

For example, news outlets repeatedly and purposely pour toxic thoughts into our brains, making us see terror or disaster around every corner. Seeing repeated scary images activates our brains' primitive fear circuits (in the amygdala). Unless you purposefully monitor your news intake, these companies succeed in raising your stress hormones, which you now know shrink the major mood and memory centers in your brain.

Granted, we do need *some* anxiety to be happy. Appropriate anxiety helps us make better decisions. It prevents us from running into the street as children, risking broken bodies, and running headlong into toxic relationships as adults, risking broken hearts.

But if you want to lower your stress level, start monitoring the amount of time you spend watching the news. Just a few minutes of negative news in the morning can lower your happiness later in the day by 27 percent,[5] so instead of turning on the TV or scrolling through your smartphone for the latest news the second you wake up, try spending a few quiet moments meditating or in prayer. Tell yourself, *Today is going to be a great day*, then lace up your sneakers and go for a brisk walk to get your blood circulating. Trust me, your brain will thank you for it!

KNOW YOUR BRAIN TYPE

WHY DO YOU DO WHAT YOU DO?

What makes you happy?

To answer these questions, it is critical to know your brain type. At Amen Clinics, we have identified five primary brain types:

1. Balanced

2. Spontaneous

3. Persistent

4. Sensitive

5. Cautious

To help you get the most out of this book, I encourage you to take our free brain type quiz at brainhealthassessment.com/. It will only take five to seven minutes, and in addition to knowing your brain type, you will also get scores on important areas of brain health.

No matter what your type is, this assessment tool will help you understand your strengths and vulnerabilities and show you how to optimize your overall brain health and happiness. When your brain works right, regardless of your brain type, you tend to work right, and that leads to a happier life.

The Balanced Brain

If you have the Balanced Brain Type, then you are a focused, flexible, and emotionally stable individual. You show up on time for meetings. You do what you say and say what you do. You don't like to take big risks and prefer to follow the rules. You're not the type to color outside the lines. Your coping skills are formidable, and you know how to go with the flow.

Balanced types don't struggle with acting

impulsively. They think about the consequences of their actions and are equipped with an inner five-second delay that keeps them from blurting out inappropriate comments. In addition, they're not the sort to mope around the house all day long. Optimists at heart, they see the glass as half-full.

Eating a balanced diet, exercising regularly, engaging in meditation or prayer, getting massages, and generally taking care of your brain and body are essential. You can support Brain Type 1 health by taking a broad-spectrum multivitamin with a strong mineral complex. Key as well are the omega-3 fatty acids found in highly potent and ultrapurified fish oils. And don't forget vitamin D, which plays many roles in regulating brain health, including keeping cognitive function in older adults.

The Spontaneous Brain

Spontaneous Brain Types can be the life of the party. They're the ones who love trying new things, get a thrill from skydiving or bungee jumping, and are willing to walk away from a secure job to throw the dice on starting their own business.

Restless and easily distracted, they need to be highly interested, excited, or stimulated in what they're doing if they're going to focus on a task set in front of them. Think firefighters and race car drivers. Organization can be a struggle for them too, and I can almost guarantee you that they won't show up on time for anything. Smokers and heavy coffee drinkers tend to fit this type, as they use these substances to turn their brains on.

Brain Type 2 can be associated with lower levels of dopamine, which may cause people to be more restless and willing to take needless risks. In order to make dopamine, your body needs tyrosine, which can be found in almonds, bananas, avocados, eggs, beans, fish, chicken, and dark chocolate. Note: Dark chocolate seems to balance all the chemicals of happiness.

The Persistent Brain

If you have the Persistent Brain Type, you like to get up in the morning and attack the day. You want to get things done, checking off items on your to-do list as you complete each task. You refuse to take no for an answer, and you go through life with a "my way or the highway" attitude. This is why others may see you as argumentative. You thrive when things go your way but get bent out of shape when something unexpected happens. You have trouble adjusting on the fly. You may be a worrier who has trouble letting go of past hurts.

Persistent types are often associated with lower levels of serotonin, which leads to struggles with obsessions and compulsions. To boost serotonin levels (which are associated with better moods), increase your intake of tryptophan. Foods such as turkey, chicken, fish, carrots, blueberries, pumpkin seeds, sweet potatoes, and garbanzo beans help drive tryptophan into the brain, where serotonin is made. Also, be aware that caffeine and diet pills tend to worsen the negative traits in Persistent people because this brain type does not need more stimulation.

The Sensitive Brain

Are you an emotional sponge, absorbing others' feelings in your own body? Then there's a strong chance that you're Sensitive. You have a way of sensing and feeling emotions that many people aren't capable of. Because of your brain type, someone else's pain and happiness become part of your pain and happiness, part of your experience.

Sensitive people typically shy away from crowds. Their idea of a lovely Saturday afternoon is more likely to involve a book of poetry, a quiet walk through a deserted forest, or traipsing through an uncrowded park or nature reserve.

Sensitive people are happiest when they can chill out. They would rather spend a quiet night at home than meet a dozen friends at a crowded pizzeria. They aren't usually fans of small talk and prefer to dive deeper with people. They don't want to be "scheduled" all the time, preferring some wiggle room or unplanned gaps in their days.

A long shower and plenty of time to get ready is heaven to Sensitives. So is having time to write in a personal journal or spend time with a book that recharges their spiritual batteries.

The Cautious Brain

If you are a Cautious Brain Type, you have high standards (for yourself and others), analyze issues in great detail before taking action, and are thorough and reliable. When you say you'll do something, you do it and do it well.

Security, safety, and predictability are important to you. You often look to the future with trepidation, but when you are wrapped up in the future, it means you are missing out on the present and live with a baseline level of anxiety, which creates misery.

Feeling a lack of control is a sticking point for many Cautious types. They are also more vulnerable to panic attacks, so pay attention when you start to sink into worst-case scenarios. Don't allow anxiety to take charge. Put an immediate halt to rising anxious thoughts with deep breathing so you can reassess the situation. Take a nice relaxing bath, enjoy a cup of chamomile tea, spend 20 minutes in quiet prayer or meditation, and watch all that stress melt away.

Now that you know your brain type, let's talk about what you can do to minimize the things that hurt your brain and steal your happiness, and optimize the things that make your brain healthier and you happier!

11 ESSENTIAL STRATEGIES TO OPTIMIZE YOUR BRAIN

THE FOUNDATIONAL SECRET to happiness is that you must first optimize the physical functioning of your brain. You do this by implementing 11 simple but effective strategies. To help you remember these strategies, I created the mnemonic BRIGHT MINDS:

Improve **B**lood Flow
Slow **R**etirement and Aging
Reduce **I**nflammation
Know **G**enetics
Avoid **H**ead Trauma
Reduce Exposure to **T**oxins

Treat **M**ental Health Issues

Optimize **I**mmunity and Prevent **I**nfections

Balance Your **N**eurohormones

Prevent **D**iabesity

Get Good **S**leep

I have written extensively about these strategies in *Memory Rescue* and *The End of Mental Illness*, so I will only summarize the main points here.

Blood Flow

Blood brings nourishment to every cell in your body and takes away waste products, so anything that damages blood vessels also damages your brain. Low blood flow is associated with depression, but when you *improve* blood flow to the brain, it can make you happier. How do you improve blood flow?

- Hydrate. Your brain is 80 percent water.
- Limit caffeine and nicotine. Both constrict blood flow to the brain.
- Exercise, even if it's just a brisk 15-minute walk every day.
- Take ginkgo biloba supplements.

- Watch a comedy. Laughing while viewing funny movies increases vascular function.[6]

Retirement and Aging

Brain imaging work reveals that your brain typically becomes less and less active with age. To slow retirement and aging, research shows that these strategies can help:

- Lifelong learning and memory training programs.
- Being socially connected and volunteering.
- Meditating.
- Taking a daily multivitamin.
- Eating foods that contain vitamin C, such as strawberries and red bell peppers.

Inflammation

You may know that too much inflammation is associated with cancer and arthritis, but did you know that it is also linked to depression? You can control a number of important and surprising causes of chronic inflammation:

- Eliminate sugar and processed foods. Get your food right, and your mind will follow.

- Floss! Poor oral health has been linked to depression and anxiety.[7] You must floss and take care of your teeth.

- Take probiotics. Maintaining good gut health is critical to lowering inflammation.

- Think positively! Being able to point to frequent moments of positivity throughout the day is associated with lower levels of inflammation.[8]

Genetics

A 2015 study in *Behavior Genetics* found that genetics accounted for about one-third of a person's life satisfaction.[9]

- If you think you're at genetic risk for brain issues, early screening is essential.

- Test your genes with 23andMe or other genetic testing services to know your vulnerabilities and meet with a medical professional to help you interpret the results.

- Take responsibility for your happiness. If 40 percent of your sense of well-being lies in genetics, that means 60 percent is in your hands.

Head Trauma

Head injuries, even mild ones that occurred decades ago, are a major cause of depression. If you've had a head injury, the good news is that many things can help it heal, even years later. Practicing the BRIGHT MINDS strategies has been shown to bring about significant improvement in blood flow, mood, memory, attention, and sleep. And when you feel better, have better recall, and sleep better, you are happier.

Toxins

Toxins are some of the most common causes of depression, anxiety, brain fog, and irritability. Many things are toxic to your brain, such as drugs, alcohol, smoking, mold exposure, carbon monoxide, and heavy metals like mercury and lead.

To decrease your toxic risk: limit your exposure whenever you can; buy organic foods to decrease pesticide consumption; avoid ingredients like phthalates, parabens, and aluminum; drink more water; eat plenty of fiber; and get plenty of exercise (sweat the bad stuff out).

Mental Health Issues

Untreated mental health issues, such as depression, anxiety, OCD, ADD/ADHD, addictions, and chronic stress hurt the brain and make you unhappy. If you struggle with any of these issues, it's critical to get them treated by a professional.

Also, if you're struggling with anxiety, the most common mental health disorder, try the following:

- Check for low blood sugar, anemia, and hyperthyroidism, as these can cause anxiety.
- Meditation and slow, deep belly breathing can immediately increase a sense of calmness.
- Calming exercises such as yoga can help.
- Start with nutritional supplements like L-theanine, GABA, and magnesium

before resorting to antianxiety medications that are hard to stop.

Immunity and Infections

When your immune system is weak, you're more likely to get infections. When it's overactive, you increase your risk for depression, anxiety, and even psychosis, and having any kind of illness saps the joy out of your life. Some of the best ways to strengthen your immunity include:

- Optimizing your Vitamin D level.
- Taking probiotics, because gut health is critical to your immunity.
- Trying an elimination diet for a month to see if food allergies may be damaging your immune system (eliminate gluten, dairy, corn, soy, sugar and artificial sweeteners, dyes, and preservatives).

Neurohormone Issues

Without healthy hormones, you feel temperamental, tired, and foggy. To keep your hormones healthy:

- Test them every year after the age of 40.
- Avoid animal proteins that were raised with hormones or antibiotics.
- Add fiber to decrease unhealthy estrogens.
- Lift weights and limit sugar to boost testosterone.
- Use hormone replacement when needed.

Diabesity

Excessive fat disrupts your hormones, stores toxins, and produces chemicals that increase inflammation. When obesity is combined with diabetes, the risk is worse. High blood sugar levels damage your blood vessels. Research shows that obesity increases the odds of depression,[10] and some studies indicate that the risk of depression doubles for those with diabetes.[11] To get diabesity under control, you have to eat healthy foods and exercise regularly (more on this later).

Sleep

When you sleep, your brain cleans or washes itself. If sleep is disrupted, trash builds up in your brain. If you want to improve your brain and feel better tomorrow, improve your sleep tonight. To sleep better:

- Make your room cooler, darker, and quieter.
- Turn off your gadgets so they don't disturb you.
- Listen to music with a slow, relaxing rhythm.
- If bad thoughts keep you awake, journal to get them out of your head.

To be happy, you must take good care of your brain. Use the BRIGHT MINDS approach to get and keep your brain healthy.

NATURAL WAYS TO FEEL GOOD

NUTRACEUTICALS (science-based natural supplements) can have a significant impact on our overall health and mood. The four basic nutraceuticals that everyone needs to be happy are:

1. **Multivitamins/minerals.** According to the Centers for Disease Control and Prevention (CDC), about 90 percent of Americans fail to consume five servings of fruits and vegetables a day,[12] the bare minimum required to get adequate amounts of nutrients. That's why everyone should take a broad-spectrum multivitamin/mineral supplement daily.

Dozens of studies in the past few decades have reported mental health benefits from multivitamin/mineral formulas consisting of more than 20 minerals and vitamins.[13] In a 2020 review of the science on broad-spectrum nutritional supplements for the treatment of certain mental health issues, 16 of 23 studies showed positive effects for symptoms of depression, anxiety, or stress.[14]

2. **Vitamin D.** This vitamin is critical for building bones and boosting the immune system, but it also is essential for a healthy brain, mood, and memory. Low levels have been associated with depression, Alzheimer's disease, heart disease, diabetes, cancer, and obesity. Ninety-three percent of the population is low in vitamin D because we are spending more time indoors and using more sunscreen (your skin absorbs the vitamin from the sun).

   One study examined vitamin D supplementation in subjects who were between 18 and 43 years old and found that those who took vitamin D reported higher positive emotions, such as being enthusiastic, excited, and determined.[15]

You should know your vitamin D level like you should know your blood pressure on a regular basis. It is a simple blood test. If it is suboptimal, take between 2,000 and 5,000 IUs a day and recheck after two months to make sure it is in the healthy range.

3. **Omega-3 fatty acids.** When it comes to overall health and well-being, omega-3 fatty acids are essential. The human body doesn't produce omega-3s on its own, so you have to get them from outside sources. For example, studies show that eating seafood with high levels of omega-3 fatty acids is correlated to a lower risk of depression and suicide. Other omega-3-rich foods include: flaxseeds, walnuts, salmon, sardines, beef, shrimp, walnut oil, chia seeds, avocados, and avocado oil.

4. **Probiotics (means "for life").** If you're not happy, the reason may not be related to your brain or mind. Your gut is often referred to as the "second brain." You have about 30 feet of

tubing that goes from your mouth to the other end. This tubing is lined with a single layer of cells with tight junctions that seal the tubing and allow you to digest your food efficiently without partly digested stuff seeping into your abdomen. Big trouble happens when the lining becomes excessively porous, a condition known as leaky gut. Leaky gut is associated with depression, anxiety disorders, and even Alzheimer's disease.

In large part, the health of your gut depends on bugs (bacteria, yeast, and others). When the ratio of good bugs to bad bugs is about 85 percent good guys to 15 percent trouble-makers, it creates a healthy gut. When the bad guys outnumber the good ones, the bad bugs cause trouble that can lead to intestinal and mental problems. Many everyday things can kill off the good bugs and tip the balance in favor of the bad guys, such as sugar and high fructose corn syrup, gluten, insomnia, toxins, low levels of vitamin D, and excessive alcohol.

By avoiding the things that fuel the growth of bad bugs, you can enhance the health of your gut, improve your mental well-being, and increase your chances of feeling good.

HAPPY FOODS VS. SAD FOODS

ONE OF THE SEVEN SECRETS to happiness is to enjoy the real happy foods (and beverages) that make you feel better, while eliminating the sad foods (and beverages) that make you feel worse.

The happy foods are the ones that make you feel good in the moment but also enhance your mood, energy, and physical well-being in the long run. This one simple eating strategy is the most important with respect to happiness.

Happy Foods

Foods that make you happy now . . . *and* later include:

- Organic colorful fruits and vegetables, especially berries and leafy greens
- Sustainably raised fish and meat
- Nuts and seeds
- Healthy oils
- Organic foods
- Low-glycemic foods (they don't spike blood sugar)
- High-fiber foods

Nuts, Seeds, Nut and Seed Butter, and Meal

Almonds, raw	Flax seeds
Brazil nuts	Pistachios
Cacao, raw	Pumpkin seeds
Cashews	Quinoa
Chia seeds	Sesame seeds
Coconut	Walnuts
Flax meal	

Legumes (small amounts, all high in fiber and protein, help balance blood sugar)

Black beans	Kidney beans
Chickpeas	Lentils
Green peas	Navy beans
Hummus	Pinto beans

Fruits (choose low-glycemic, high-fiber varieties)

Acai berries
Apples
Apricots
Avocados
Blackberries
Blueberries
Cantaloupe
Cherries
Cranberries
Figs
Goji berries
Grapefruit
Grapes (red and green)
Honeydew melon
Kiwi
Kumquat
Lemons
Lychee
Nectarines
Olives
Oranges
Passion fruit
Peaches
Pears
Plums
Pomegranates
Pumpkin
Raspberries
Strawberries
Tangerines
Tomatoes

Vegetables

Artichokes
Asparagus
Beets and beet greens
Bell peppers
Broccoli
Brussels sprouts
Butternut squash
Cabbage
Carrots
Cauliflower
Celery

Collard greens
Cucumber
Garlic
Green beans
Jicama
Kale
Leeks
Mustard greens
Okra
Onions
Parsley
Parsnips
Red or green leaf lettuce
Romaine lettuce
Scallions
Seaweed
Spinach
Spirulina
Summer squash
Sweet potatoes
Swiss chard
Turnips
Watercress
Zucchini

Oils

Avocado oil
Coconut oil (stable at high temperatures)
Macadamia nut oil
Olive oil (stable only at room temperature)

Eggs, Meat, Poultry, and Fish

Chicken or turkey
Eggs
King crab
Lamb (high in omega-3s)
Rainbow trout
Salmon, wild caught
Scallops
Shrimp

Brain-Healthy Herbs and Spices

Basil	Nutmeg
Black pepper	Oregano
Cayenne pepper	Parsley
Cinnamon	Peppermint
Cloves	Rosemary
Curcumin	Saffron
Garlic	Sage
Ginger	Thyme
Marjoram	Turmeric
Mint	

The Standard American Diet (aptly referred to as "SAD") is filled with foods that are loaded with unhealthy ingredients and artificial chemicals that are detrimental to mental, emotional, and physical well-being. A growing body of research shows that the SAD diet increases your risk for depression and anxiety disorders, as well as diabetes, hypertension, heart disease, and cancer.[16]

Sad Foods

I call these the weapons of mass destruction because they are destroying the health of America, and we are exporting these food patterns around the world. These are foods that make you happy now but make you feel bad, tired, anxious, or stressed later, including those that are:

- Highly processed
- Sprayed with pesticides
- High-glycemic foods (they spike blood sugar)
- Low in fiber
- Food-like substances
- Artificially colored and sweetened
- Laden with hormones
- Tainted with antibiotics
- Stored in plastic containers

Happy Beverages

Don't forget, your brain is composed of approximately 80 percent water, and it needs adequate hydration for you to feel your best. Being even slightly dehydrated can mess with your mood and more, making you feel more depressed, anxious, tense, angry, or hostile, in addition to draining your energy, increasing pain, and lowering your ability to concentrate.[17]

To stay properly hydrated, drink eight to ten

glasses of water a day. But guzzling isn't the only way to ensure you are keeping your brain well-lubed. Consuming water-rich foods, such as vegetables and fruits, can help you reach your fluid needs. Healthy sources of hydration include

- Water
- Sparkling water (add a splash of chocolate or orange stevia [brand: SweetLeaf] for a refreshing, calorie-free, and toxin-free "soda")
- Spa water (sparkling water with berries, a sprig of mint, or a slice of lemon, orange, peach, or melon)
- Herbal tea
- Unsweetened almond milk (for amazing taste, add a few drops of flavored stevia)
- Coconut water
- Lightly flavored waters, such as Hint
- Vegetable juice or green drinks (without added fruit juice)
- Water with cayenne pepper to boost metabolism
- Beet juice (to increase blood flow)
- Cherry juice (to help sleep)

Sad Beverages

Alcohol, highly caffeinated drinks (coffee, energy drinks, sodas), and high-sodium beverages that restrict blood vessels.

The right foods can make you very happy, while the wrong ones can steal your joy. The choice is yours.

CONTROLLING YOUR NEGATIVE THOUGHTS

IF YOU FOCUS ON LOSS, you will feel grief.

If you focus on fear, you will feel afraid.

If you focus on gratitude, you will feel grateful.

If you focus on those who love you, you will feel loved.

If you focus on the times you have felt joy, you will feel joyful.

That's why one of the secrets to happiness is using your mind to help you rather than hurt you. Negative thoughts raise cortisol, which makes you feel anxious and depressed. Positive thoughts release dopamine and serotonin, which help you feel so much better. The good news is, you can program your brain to be happy.

The key is to "take every thought captive," as the apostle Paul wrote to the Corinthian church nearly 2,000 years ago (2 Corinthians 10:5, ESV). Taking your thoughts captive means gaining control over what you think about yourself and your life.

You can do this by using four simple strategies:

1. **Play the "Glad Game" (see day 18).** When it comes to being happy, it's critical to look for what makes you happy rather than continually seeking whatever makes you sad, anxious, or afraid. So, no matter what situation or setback you find yourself in, I urge you to ask yourself this question: What is there to be glad about?

2. **Give your mind a name.** Most of us live with a constant stream of "intrusive" internal thoughts and criticisms from the past bouncing around our brains. You can train yourself to dismiss intrusive thoughts by giving your internal voice a name that you don't call yourself so it's different from "you." I named my brain Hermie after the pet raccoon I had as a

kid. Hermie was a troublemaker, just like my mind. Even after all these years as a psychiatrist, Hermie can still cause trouble by saying things like "You're a failure" or "You're an idiot." When this happens, I metaphorically put Hermie in a cage for a while.

Years of research show that "distanced self-talk" can help someone gain psychological distance from intrusive thoughts, helping them better regulate their emotions, self-control, and wisdom.[18] People are better able to handle negative emotions and intense situations, even if they previously struggled to manage their feelings or behavior.

As humans, we have the ability for self-reflection, which helps us plan for the future and solve complex problems, but when we perceive bad experiences are happening, self-reflection can turn into the darkness of negativity, rumination, or obsession. Distancing ourselves from the negative chatter in our minds by giving our minds a name—or talking to ourselves in the third person—can bring in more reality and positively change our brains. What would you name your mind?

3. **Interrupt unnecessary unhappy moments.** When unnecessary unhappy moments come up, spend a few seconds feeling bad. Go to the dark place. Let the bad feeling wash over you. After you feel bad, say, "Stop," stand up, and take three deep breaths. By doing this, you create space where a void will take shape. Then, fill the void with happy memories so you can feel good on purpose. Finally, wire the good feeling into your nervous system by celebrating your ability to interrupt the unnecessary unhappy moments. Celebrating is essential to making new habits stick. You'll learn more about this on day 16.

4. **Feel great anytime, anywhere.** Anchor your happiest memories to specific places in your brain that you already know, such as rooms or objects in your home so you can easily recall them (for example, you may attach a specific memory of your mom baking cookies to the oven in your kitchen). You can literally associate hundreds of things with the insides of most homes.

   With a little practice, this exercise can help you feel amazing anytime, anywhere.

FOCUS ON BEHAVIORS YOU LIKE

WHAT IF I WERE TO TELL YOU that you had the power to change the way people treat you? No, really! You do! Here's how I know. . . .

One day a 16-year-old patient stormed into my office, sat on the couch, and told me that she hated her mother and was running away from home. Her mother had untreated ADD/ADHD and tended to pick on Jessie as a way to stimulate her own brain.

In the middle of the rant, she turned her anger on me. "Tell me, Dr. Amen. Why does a grown man collect penguins?"

In my office at the time were hundreds of penguins—pens, dolls, puppets, etc. I laughed and said, "Let me tell you the story.

"A long time ago, when my son was seven, he was difficult for me. As a way to work on our relationship, I took him to a sea animal park. We had fun at the whale show and the sea lion show, and at the end of the day my son wanted to see the penguin show. The penguin's name was Fat Freddy. He was an amazing chubby little penguin. He dove off a high diving board, bowled with his nose, counted with his flippers, and jumped through a hoop of fire. Then, toward the end of the show, the trainer asked Freddy to go get something, and Freddy went and brought the item right back.

"*Wow*, I thought to myself. *I ask this kid to get something for me, and he wants to have a discussion for twenty minutes, and then he doesn't want to do it.* I knew my son was smarter than the penguin.

"So, after the show, I went up to the trainer and asked her how she got Freddy to do all of those really cool things. The trainer looked at my son and then at me and said, 'Unlike parents, whenever Freddy does something I want him to do, I notice him. I give him a hug, and I give him a fish.'

"Even though my son didn't like whole raw fish, a light turned on in my head. Whenever my son did things that I liked, I paid no attention to him at all because, like my own father, I was a busy guy. But when he didn't do what I wanted him to do, I gave him a ton of attention because I didn't want to raise bad children. I was inadvertently teaching him to act badly in order to get my attention. So now I collect penguins as a way to remind myself to notice the good things about the people in my life a lot more than the bad things."[19]

As I finished telling the story, I got a crazy idea. What if my patient could shape her mother's behavior the same way the trainer shaped Freddy's by ignoring negative interactions and rewarding positive ones?

"I know this will be hard," I told her, "but whenever your mother starts in on you, don't challenge her or get emotional. Then whenever she is nice to you, listens to you, is more appropriate with you, tell her how much you love and appreciate her."

Jessie was skeptical but agreed to give it a try.

That night, I got a text from her saying that she decided not to run away from home. A week later, she said our plan was working. Two weeks after that, when I saw her again, she said things were much better at home, and she brought me a penguin to add to my collection.

You have the power to make your relationships with your loved ones better or worse. Why not opt for the happier, less stressful route?

MICRO-MOMENTS OF HAPPINESS

OVER THE YEARS, I've seen many patients who feel disconnected and insignificant. They lack a sense of meaning and purpose. They lack a relationship with God or something bigger than themselves. Regardless of religion, denomination, or even personal belief in God, without a spiritual connection, many people experience an underlying sense of despair or meaninglessness. At their core, they are unhappy. It doesn't have to be that way.

We are all spiritual beings created with divine purpose, whether or not we believe in God. Each person has a role to play in the lives of those around them and a mission to fulfill. Having a deep sense of meaning and purpose gives you a reason to get up in the morning.

Purpose gives you a sense of what matters most in the grand scheme of life and eternity, and it is essential for happiness. Without knowing your purpose, it's hard to have values and goals that matter. When you make decisions based on your purpose, it shifts your focus away from self and onto others.

Let me ask you a question: Why is the world a better place because you breathe? If you don't know the answer to this question, think it over. Ask those closest to you for their insights. What skills do you have that could be helpful to someone today? What can you do to make the world a better place?

Knowing your purpose guides your goals and decisions in what I call the Four Circles—the four areas of your life that make up the essence of who you are:

- **Biological Circle:** how your physical body and brain function

- **Psychological Circle:** developmental issues and how you think
- **Social Circle:** social support, your current life situation, and societal influences
- **Spiritual Circle:** your connection to God, the planet, past and future generations, and your deepest sense of meaning and purpose

If you were one of my patients, I'd ask you to do an exercise to identify what makes you happy in each of the Four Circles. And bear in mind, we're not talking about major life-changing events. I'm talking about finding joy in the small things, like hearing a bird sing outside your window, feeling the warmth of the sun on your face when you step outside, or petting your dog or cat. I call these micro-moments of happiness. Most of us gloss over these little things, searching instead for the big experiences. I want you to savor these precious times because when your brain pays attention to them, they add up to more overall contentment and satisfaction with your life. The more micro-moments you cherish, the greater your sense of joy.

For example:

Biological Micro-Moments: the first sip of a brain-healthy cappuccino or hot chocolate, the first bite of an orange, the taste of guacamole made from fresh avocados, or hearing a song you love

Psychological Micro-Moments: making a great play in a Sudoku puzzle, laughing at a joke or funny scene in a movie or TV show, listening to a cool plot twist in an audiobook, or putting words together to make someone laugh

Social Micro-Moments: hearing a loved one's voice on the phone, getting a fun text from a friend, or hugging a friend you haven't seen in a while

Spiritual Micro-Moments: saying a prayer each night, randomly remembering a Bible verse that applies to a situation you are in, or being grateful for another day

I urge you to do your own Four Circles of Happiness exercise. Within each circle, write down what makes you happy while keeping these questions in mind:

What brings a smile to your face?
What makes you feel good about life?
What do you value most?

When you have finished, look at how many things you have listed in each circle. Does one circle have a much shorter list? Are you out of balance in any of these areas? If so, you may be neglecting one of your circles. Be sure to look at your Four Circles of Happiness every day as a way to remind yourself about the things that bring you joy.

Focusing on doing what you love to do is a surefire way to make you happier.

AT THE CORE OF YOUR HAPPINESS

WHAT ARE CORE VALUES, and why are they key to your happiness? Core values are the character- istics or traits you think are most important in the way you live. They help you make decisions when you are faced with challenging situations. For example, let's say you are training to run a marathon, but on the morning of one of your long training runs, your child gets a tummy ache. Do you forego your run to care for your child? What if you have a rehearsal dinner for your best friend's wedding, but your supervisor at work hands you a last-minute project that needs to be done *stat!* The decisions you make come from your core values. Knowing which core values are most important to you helps guide you to the decisions that fit with your life goals.

Here's how to clarify your core values in just three steps.

Step 1: Choose one or two of the following characteristics or traits that are important to you in each of the Four Circles. Feel free to add your own.

BIOLOGICAL	PSYCHOLOGICAL	SOCIAL	SPIRITUAL
Athleticism	Authenticity	Caring	Acceptance
Beauty	Confidence	Connection	Appreciation
Brain/body love	Courage	Dependability	Awareness (awe)
Brain health	Creativity	Empathy	Compassion
Energy	Flexibility	Encouragement	Generosity
Fitness	Forthrightness	Family	Gratitude
Focus	Fun	Friendships	Growth
Longevity	Happiness/joy	Independence	Humility
Mental clarity	Hard work	Kindness	Inspiration
Physical health	Individuality	Love of others	Love/relationship with God
Safety	Open-mindedness	Loyalty	Morality
Strength	Positivity	Outcome-driven/service	Patience
Vitality	Resilience	Passion	Prayerful
	Responsibility	Significance	Purposeful

BIOLOGICAL	PSYCHOLOGICAL	SOCIAL	SPIRITUAL
	Science-based	Success	Religious community
	Security	Tradition	Surrender
	Self-control		Transcendence
	Self-love		Wonder

Step 2: Think of six to eight heroes (past and present) you admire most and write down the values you think represent their lives. Your heroes can be people you know personally, public figures, or even entities (such as a fire department, sports team, or school)—anyone who has inspired you in some important way.

Step 3: Review your values. Over time, observe yourself and pay attention to the decisions you make and why. What values do they reflect and how do they impact your life? Write them down and post them where you can see them often. Make it a habit to review your values from time to time to see if they still resonate with you or if you should update them. Do they reflect the values you want?

Staying focused on your core values will help you make better decisions. And better decisions are essential to happiness.

KNOW YOUR PURPOSE IN SIX QUESTIONS

BELIEVING YOUR LIFE MATTERS is essential to happiness. When you know your purpose, you feel more significant, happier, and more connected. A study in the *Archives of General Psychiatry* followed more than 900 people for up to 7 years to look at the effects of having a sense of purpose, which they defined as "the psychological tendency to derive meaning from life's experiences and to possess a sense of intentionality and goal directedness that guides behavior."[20] The researchers found that the people who were more purposeful at the start of the study had:

- Greater happiness
- Less depression
- More satisfaction
- Better mental health
- Personal growth, self-acceptance
- Better quality sleep
- Longevity

This is only one of many studies linking purpose with life satisfaction and lowered mortality rates. A 27-year study concluded that living with purpose and meaning is the key to happiness and longevity.[21] Another paper in a 2015 issue of the *Lancet* measured "eudemonic well-being," a type of well-being that relates to having a sense of purpose and meaning in life, and found that it was tied to longevity.[22] Scoring higher in "purpose in life" also reduces the chances that negative social media issues (such as not having as many followers as your peers, not getting the number of likes you want, or receiving negative comments about your posts) will affect your self-esteem.[23] This body of research points to purpose as a foundational element for a happy life.

Any time I talk to my patients about purpose, I bring up Viktor Frankl, the famed psychiatrist, Holocaust survivor, and author of the remarkable book *Man's Search for Meaning*. He said that "life is never made unbearable by circumstances, but only by lack of meaning and purpose" and explored three elements of purpose:

- Purposeful work or being productive. This involves asking yourself questions such as *Why is the world a better place because I am here?* or *What do I contribute?*
- Loving other people
- Courage despite difficulty. Bearing whatever challenges you have and helping others with theirs.

To find your true purpose in life, you simply need to know where to look. To help you zero in on what gives your life meaning, write down your answers to the following questions.

1. **Look inward.** What do you love to do? Examples include writing, cooking, design, parenting, creating, speaking, teaching, and

so on. What do you feel qualified to teach others about?

2. **Look outward.** Who do you do it for? How does your work connect you to others?

3. **Look back.** Are there hurts from your past that you can turn into help for others? Turn your pain into purpose.

4. **Look beyond yourself.** What do others want or need from you?

5. **Look for transformation.** How do others change as a result of what you do?

6. **Look to the end.** Psychiatrist Elisabeth Kübler-Ross, author of the well-known book *On Death and Dying*, said, "It is the denial of death that is partially responsible for people living empty, purposeless lives; for when you live as if you'll live forever, it becomes too easy to postpone the things you know that you must do."[24] Ask yourself, *Does this worry, problem, or moment have eternal value? When I die, how do I want to be remembered?*

Notice that only two of the six questions are about you; four of them are about others. A wise Chinese saying is: "If you want happiness for an hour, take a nap. If you want happiness for a day, go fishing. If you want happiness for a year, inherit a fortune. If you want happiness for a lifetime, help someone else."[25] Happiness is often found in helping others.

TAME YOUR
INNER DRAGONS

DRAGONS. We've all got them. You have them, your significant other has them, and so do your boss, coworkers, friends, parents, siblings, and kids. They're those pesky inner beasts that breathe fire on your emotional brain and steal your happiness. Left untamed, they can run wild and drive depression, anxiety, and other emotional health issues.

Learning to recognize your dragons is the first step to taming them. You can discover which dragons you have and find out more about

their origins and triggers by taking my quiz at
KnowYourDragons.com.

When you take the quiz, you'll learn about 13
different Dragons:

**Abandoned, Invisible, or Insignificant
Dragons**—feel alone, unseen, or
unimportant

Inferior or Flawed Dragons—feel less than
others

Anxious Dragons—feel fearful and
overwhelmed

Wounded Dragons—bruised by past trauma

Should and Shaming Dragons—racked
with guilt

Special, Spoiled, or Entitled Dragons—feel
more special than others

Responsible Dragons—need to take care of
others

Angry Dragons—harbor hurts and rage

Judgmental Dragons—hold harsh or critical
opinions of others due to past injustices

Death Dragons—fear the future and lack of a meaningful life

Grief and Loss Dragons—feel loss and fear of loss

Hopeless and Helpless Dragons— have pervasive sense of despair and discouragement

Ancestral Dragons—affected by issues from past generations

The good news is that Dragons do not have to control you. You can rewrite their stories. Here are five simple steps to do just that:

1. Identify the dragons blocking your path to success and work to retrain them by looking at their triggers and upsides.

2. See yourself as the creator of your story: past, present, and future. I used to tell myself that my late father never spent any time with us. For decades, I remembered him with bitterness and believed I was justified for having those negative feelings. Then when I was 50,

he gave all his kids copies of home movies he took when we were young. It had many moments with him at the park, pool, or parties playing with us. My Insignificant and Angry Dragons had been lying to me, which had a negative impact on our relationship. Being able to rewrite the story from a more accurate, mature standpoint dramatically helped our relationship while he was still alive, as well as how I felt inside.

3. Know what you want. Write it down and ask yourself, *What can I do today to start getting what I want?* You don't have to do everything today, just one small thing. I often tell my patients who feel frozen by fear that they don't have to react all at once, just move their pinky finger to signal they can do something.

4. Remember that where you focus your attention always determines how you feel. If I focused on my critics, I would feel criticized, angry, small, and like a victim. If I focus on all the people we've helped, I feel happy and

purposeful. I have a choice on the arc and ending of the story.

5. Realize it is never too late to change your story. Start today. As the title character in the film *The Curious Case of Benjamin Button* said, "It's never too late . . . to be whoever you wanna be. . . . You can change or stay the same. There are no rules to this thing. . . . I hope you live a life you're proud of, and if you find that you're not, I hope you have the strength to start all over again."[26]

Trust me . . . once you get your dragons under control, you'll be a lot happier!

A LITTLE TLC
GOES A LONG WAY

HOW IS IT THAT SOME PEOPLE seem to be so happy even though the world is falling apart? How come some people can survive the most horrific situations while others struggle? Researchers have found that in high-stress cases, people who can't weather the storm typically believe three things:

- The situation is *permanent.*
- The situation is *global.*
- They have *no control* over the situation.

There is a technique that I tell my patients to use whenever they feel stressed and anxious because it actually flips your thinking to being more hopeful about the future. The technique is called TLC:

- The situation is *temporary*.
- The situation is *local*.
- You have some *control* over the situation.

Here's how it works. I think we can all agree that the COVID-19 pandemic was a very difficult, stressful time. Well, let's run it through the TLC filter and see if we can't find a more positive way of looking at it:

Temporary: The coronavirus pandemic will not last forever. Think about all the pandemics from the past—the Spanish influenza, bubonic plague, and cholera, for example. They all eventually resolved. This will pass too. And every time our economy has dipped into a recession, it has rebounded.

Local: Although COVID-19 cases have been reported worldwide, the illness has not hit every street in every neighborhood in every city in every country of the world. While far too many died, the vast majority of those who contracted the virus survived. Even though my dad died not long after contracting the virus, my mom and a few other family members survived it, and many of my friends and colleagues never got it.

Control: What can I do to "control" the spread of the coronavirus? Practice good hygiene and shore up my immune system with vitamins D and C and with zinc.

For managing the control aspect of TLC, I often say the Serenity Prayer, attributed to American theologian Reinhold Niebuhr.[27] It is the essence of mental health:

> *God, grant me the serenity to*
> *accept the things I cannot change,*
> *the courage to change the things I can,*
> *and the wisdom to know the difference.*

Practicing TLC by walking yourself through what is temporary, what is local, and what you can control will strengthen your resilience to get through any significant issue in your life.

DAY 13

DON'T LET ANTS RUIN YOUR PICNIC

EARLY IN MY PRACTICE, I treated a lot of patients complaining about deep, dark, negative thoughts, or what I call ANTs (automatic negative thoughts). There are nine types of ANTs that can infest your mind, like pests at a Fourth of July picnic:

The All-or-Nothing ANTs. There's no in-between for these ANTs. Things are either all good or all bad—and usually bad. They rely on adverbs like *always* and *never*: *I always mess up. . . . I'll never lose weight.*

The Less-Than ANTs. These ANTs continuously compare themselves to others and see themselves as coming up short. They damage your self-esteem by reminding you that you don't measure up, which makes you feel less than your friends and acquaintances.

The Just-the-Bad ANTs. These ANTs go out of their way to see the bad in every situation. They are the people who, when they learn about an unexpected inheritance, will complain about the taxes they have to pay.

The Guilt-Beating ANTs. These ANTs are mired in the words *should, must, ought,* or *have to.* People with these ANTs readily recall their miscues, bad decisions, and stupid stuff they said. They replay a litany of shortcomings they heard from parents and authority figures.

The Labeling ANTs. When you call yourself a loser, you have a labeling ANT in your brain. The problem with labeling yourself with a negative term is that it can become a self-fulfilling prophecy.

The Fortune-Telling ANTs. These ANTs predict the worst in any situation and then make the situation worse still.

The Mind-Reading ANTs. These ANTs are convinced they can see into someone else's mind and know *exactly* what that person is thinking about them—like how stupid they are. But just as you can't read other people's minds, other people can't read yours.

The If-Only and I'll-Be-Happy-When ANTs. These ANTs tend to wallow in regret, repeating "If only" as an excuse for why they don't have the life they want. *If only I had more money . . . if only I were skinnier . . . if only I'd never married the bum . . .* And if you think you'll be happier *when you get that promotion, when you move into a bigger house, when you get married*—it just prevents you from finding ways to be happy now.

The Blaming ANTs. Of all the ANTs, this one is the worst because blaming others often results in taking little to no responsibility for your life. Since you consider yourself to be a victim of others' negative actions, you feel powerless to change your behavior.

Most people don't know that positive and negative thoughts release different chemicals in the brain. Whenever you have a happy thought, a bright idea, or a loving feeling, your brain releases the chemicals of happiness, such as dopamine, serotonin, and endorphins that calm the body. Whenever you have a negative thought, the brain releases or decreases chemicals, leaving you angry, sad, or stressed out. The release of stress hormones, cortisol (the molecule of danger) and adrenaline, and the depletion of feel-good neurotransmitters, dopamine and serotonin, changes your body's chemistry and brain's focus. This makes you unhappy.

When dealing with ANTs, the best defense is a good offense. That's why developing a positivity bias in your mindset can counterbalance the mind's tendency to focus on the negative.

Whenever you feel sad, mad, nervous, or out of control, write down what you are thinking and ask yourself if it is true. To kill the ANTs, write down your negative thoughts, identify which ANT species they are, and challenge them by asking yourself five questions that I learned from my friend, author Byron Katie.[28]

1. Is it true?

2. Is it absolutely true with 100 percent certainty?

3. How do you feel when you believe that thought?

4. How would you feel if you didn't have that thought?

5. Turn the thought around to its opposite and ask if the opposite is true. Is there any evidence that it is true?

If you challenge your thoughts to achieve a more positive outlook, you'll be able to keep those ANT infestations under control.

LAUGHTER
IS THE BEST MEDICINE

WANT TO INJECT A LITTLE POSITIVITY into your life? Laugh more. Every time you let out a chuckle, your brain releases the chemicals of happiness—dopamine, oxytocin, and endorphins—while lowering the stress hormone cortisol. A hearty laugh is like a drug, changing your brain chemistry to make you feel happier, and making it happen almost instantly.

So what is laughter, and how does it happen? Laughter shows emotion, such as mirth, joy, or scorn with a chuckle or explosive vocal sound.

What this definition lacks is where laughter

starts, and that's the brain. We know that the left side of the brain is responsible for interpreting words, including jokes. The brain's right side is responsible for identifying what makes the joke, observation, or situation funny. The brain's prefrontal cortex is responsible for emotional responses, but the basal ganglia—the area of the brain that integrates movement and emotion—becomes active when we're watching a funny movie or sitcom on TV. These areas produce the physical actions of laughing.

The best thing about laughter is how good it is for you. A Loma Linda University study on the effect of laughter showed that hilarity and mirth release endorphins—the body's painkillers—and lower blood pressure.[29] As the old proverb goes, laughter is the best medicine, and "humor is mankind's greatest blessing"—a famous saying attributed to Mark Twain.

So how can you laugh more? Well, laughter is contagious, so if you and your friends are able to take in a comedy at the movies, visit a local comedy club, or watch a live production of a farce-type play, do it. If everyone is laughing together, a bond is created that makes you more likely to express your true feelings, which also has a positive effect on your life.

In their book, *Humor, Seriously*, Jennifer Aaker and Naomi Bagdonas write that using humor to make other people laugh can be just as beneficial, helping us appear more intelligent, deepening bonds, enhancing creativity, and strengthening resilience.[30] So how can you make others laugh if you weren't born with a natural funny bone? With practice, even you can find your wittiness by using two common elements of humor:

A foundation in the truth
The unexpected

I often use these two principles of humor in my clinical practice as well as in my books and public television shows. It allows me to deliver complex information in a way that helps people understand it and remember it more easily. For example, here is something I said in my public television show *Change Your Brain, Heal Your Mind*.

I was telling the audience that it was my 14th public television show about the brain and that everywhere I go across the country people tell me how my programs have changed their lives. So I gave them the following few examples:

> I was walking recently when I saw a couple running toward me. The wife recognized me and said, "Hey, you're the brain doctor. We are out here running because of you. My husband wouldn't listen to *me*, but he listens to *you*!"
>
> I also met a flight attendant who told me that she lost 30 pounds and stopped feeling depressed since watching my shows because she completely changed her diet and was getting her husband and her children to walk with her.
>
> And I met a Stanford professor who told me he completely stopped drinking because of my programs and now wakes up feeling 100 percent every day.

Then I threw in a zinger:

> But my favorite story is of the 87-year-old woman who told me that she started

dating again after she watched my shows
because she realized that being alone was
not good for her brain. With a smile
she told me that she had recently met a
wonderful 80-year-old man online and
they were having the time of their lives.
I wondered if that qualified her as being
a grandmother cougar.

As soon as I said "grandmother cougar," the
audience burst into laughter. What I said was all
rooted in truth, but I threw in something unexpected that made the audience's brains do a
double take. And by making them laugh, my
own brain released a cocktail of feel-good neurochemicals that made me feel happy at the same
time.

GOOD NIGHTS =
HAPPIER DAYS

HOW WOULD YOUR HOME LOOK if no one cleaned it for a month? Pretty cluttered, right? That's the effect chronic insomnia can have on your brain. And nobody is their best self when they're exhausted.

Proper sleep is essential for brain health. In fact, scientists have shown that your brain cleanses or "washes" itself during sleep. You see, the brain has a special waste management system that helps get rid of toxins that build up over the course of a day. Your brain is so busy managing your life during the daylight hours that this cleaning system is pretty much turned off, and without healthy sleep, the brain's cleaning crew does not have enough time to do its job, and trash builds up, causing brain fog, elevating your risk of stroke, cardiovascular disease, anxiety, cancer, and death from any cause.[31]

Researchers suggest we aim for seven to eight hours of sleep a night; it seems to be the sweet spot for most people. Simply put, if you want to feel happier tomorrow, improve your sleep tonight.

Do this by avoiding:

- Caffeine (no caffeine after lunchtime)
- A warm room
- Light and noise, especially from your gadgets
- Alcohol. Yes, it will put you to sleep, but when it wears off, your brain will rebound and wake you up a few hours later.

To sleep better:

- Make your room cooler, darker, and quieter.
- Turn off your gadgets so they don't disturb you.

- Listen to music with a slow, relaxing rhythm (about 60 beats per minute).
- Try medical hypnosis. (Amen Clinics has a powerful program to help you retrain your brain to sleep.)
- Take magnesium and melatonin, which are often very effective, as is 5-HTP if you're a worrier.
- If you have bad thoughts that keep you awake, journal to get them out of your head.

To be happy, you must keep your brain healthy. And getting a good night's sleep is a great way to achieve both!

WHERE YOUR MIND GOES, YOUR MOOD FOLLOWS

WHEN JOSEPH McCLENDON III was a teenager, a racially motivated attack by three white men left him injured and eventually homeless. After hitting rock bottom, he somehow transformed his mindset to become a doctor of neuropsychology, a bestselling author, and a spellbinding orator who often teaches at Tony Robbins's seminars. Joseph says that when unnecessary unhappy moments come up, he takes a simple, four-step process to get back on track:

Step 1: Feel bad on purpose. Spend a few seconds feeling bad. Go to the dark place. Let the bad feeling wash over you. Sounds sort of crazy, doesn't it? But a few seconds can be empowering because if you know how to make yourself feel bad, you can also decide to interrupt it.

Step 2: Interrupt the pattern. If the bad feelings are unnecessary or unhelpful, which they often are, then interrupt them. I say "unnecessary" because some bad feelings are necessary. For me, those feelings surfaced when my grandfather and my father died and when I unintentionally said something hurtful to my wife. I needed to feel bad at those moments, and it would be inappropriate not to allow myself to feel that way. Yet, most times when I feel bad, it is unnecessary and needs to be interrupted and replaced, such as when I was attacked on the internet after a "Why I Got the Vaccine" live chat.

After you practice feeling bad, say, "Stop," stand up, and take three deep breaths. By doing this, you create space where a void will take shape. Careful, though: Voids always want to be filled, so your mind will default to negativity if you allow it; instead, direct it toward something better and more useful for yourself.

For many of my patients, I have them wear a rubber band around their wrists (like one of my favorite Lakers players, Wilt Chamberlain, did). When they feel bad, I ask them to stand up, say "Stop," snap the rubber band against their wrist, and then do several deep-breathing exercises. The physical act of standing up, creating a physical distraction, and intentionally focusing on breathing interrupts the pattern of feeling bad.

Step 3: Purposefully focus on happy memories. Fill the void with happy memories so you can feel good on purpose. Remember, where you focus your attention determines how you feel. I ask all of my patients to write down 10 to 20 of their happiest life memories. Focus on one of those nice memories until you can truly feel happy or joyful. Imagine the memory with all of your senses: See what's there, hear any sounds, feel the sensations, and smell and taste what is in the air. Do this for several minutes until you can feel the memory in your soul.

Step 4: Celebrate. Last, wire the good feeling into your nervous system by celebrating your ability to interrupt the unnecessary unhappy moments. Celebrating is essential to making new habits stick.

If you practice feeling bad, go through this simple process and begin to gain mastery over your happiness.

Joseph is so keen on dealing with unnecessary unhappy moments that he sets a timer on his smartphone so that a ringtone goes off at the top of the hour, reminding him that it's time to "visit" a bad feeling, just for an instant.

"You don't want to get mired in it or bogged down with it," he told me. "You just feel it for a couple of seconds, then stand up, put a smile on your face, snap out of it, and pat yourself on the back. Do that ten times, and it's really going to be hard to find that negative emotion again."

The step of standing up is more important than you think. When you rise to your feet, you create a scotoma—a blind spot—in the brain. It's like when you're sitting on the couch in the living room and decide that you want to read the local newspaper that's sitting on the kitchen counter.

You stand up, make your way to the kitchen, and walk in—and immediately ask yourself,

What am I looking for again? What happened is that you interrupted a pattern—sitting on the couch—and created a scotoma or blind spot. The same principle applies when you have a bad feeling: Stand up, create a scotoma for the brain, replace it with something positive, celebrate, and move on.

When you move on physically, your brain opens up, allowing you to put something else in its place—like something positive that you can "anchor" into your mind.

Joseph once said:

As you think, so you feel.
As you feel, so you do.
As you do, so you have.[32]

In other words, thoughts create feelings like happiness or anger. Feelings create our behaviors, and our behaviors create our successes or failures in our relationships, work, money, and health. It starts with brain health and then getting your thoughts to serve you rather than hurt you.

CREATE YOUR OWN SAFE HAVEN

IN THE EARLY 2000S, Dr. Ronald Ruden, an internist with a PhD in organic chemistry, developed havening, a healing technique using therapeutic touch to change pathways in the brain linked to emotional distress. Dr. Ruden theorized that certain touching techniques could help boost serotonin production in the brain, allowing us to relax and detach from an upsetting life experience. The practice of havening involves one or more of the following touch techniques:

Rubbing the palms of your hands together slowly, as if washing your hands.

Giving yourself a hug. This technique involves placing the palms of your hands on your opposite shoulders and rubbing them down your arms to your elbows.

"Washing your face" by placing your fingertips up high on your forehead, just below your hairline, and then letting your hands fall down your face to your chin.

From a neuroscience perspective, havening is a form of stimulating both sides of the brain (essential for healing) while you mentally bring up a stressful thought or past trauma.

Havening got a boost during the pandemic when singer Justin Bieber released a YouTube documentary video showing him using the touch technique. While Justin massages his temples in a hunched-over, sitting posture, his wife, Hailey, explains on camera: "It's basically a self-soothing thing . . . when you're starting to feel really stressed out or just [want to] keep yourself calm. It's almost like when you're a kid, and your mom is rubbing your back to sleep, and it's the best feeling in the world. It's kind of like that, except you're doing it for yourself."[33]

Dr. Ruden reports that his research has shown that havening generates high amplitude neural oscillations known as delta waves, which we experience when asleep.[34] Delta waves calm regions of the brain involved in creating emotionally charged memories and trauma. One of these brain regions is the amygdala, which plays a significant role in recording the emotions of our experiences.

When it comes to traumatic experiences, the amygdala encodes the related emotions differently, becoming what neuroscientists call "potentiated." This means the trauma and emotions get hardwired into your brain and stick like superglue. Havening helps loosen the glue in your brain.

LOOK FOR THE POSITIVE

I WAS JUST STARTING elementary school when Walt Disney Studios released *Pollyanna*, a feature film adapted from a popular novel about an orphan daughter of missionaries sent to live with her wealthy, stern, and unmarried aunt in the fictional town of Beldingsville, Vermont. Hayley Mills, a 14-year-old British actress with adorable blonde curls and a button nose, played the role of the title character.

Pollyanna was one of my favorite Disney films growing up. She told her friends that her departed father devised the Glad Game after she received a pair of crutches in the mail instead of the doll she wanted for Christmas—obviously a mix-up that wasn't easily rectified in 1913. What was she glad about? Well, Pollyanna said she was thankful that she didn't need the crutches.

When she went to live with Aunt Polly, Pollyanna was punished for being late for dinner and relegated to eating bread and milk in the kitchen with one of the maids. No problem— bread and milk became her favorite meal. When the spinster aunt Polly banished her to a bedroom in the attic with no pictures, rugs, or mirror, Pollyanna looked outside and decided she wouldn't have noticed the beautiful willow trees outside her window if she had pictures on the wall.

Pollyanna is quickly introduced to a grouchy old miser, a self-pitying invalid, a hypochondriac, a recluse, and a fire-and-brimstone preacher. They share one trait: They are always complaining about something. Pollyanna, however, mirrors what her missionary parents taught her: It's better to focus on the goodness of life and look for something to be glad about, no matter how dire or bleak the situation is.

One Sunday afternoon, Pollyanna is hanging out in the backyard of Aunt Polly's Victorian mansion, listening to Tillie (the house cook), Angie and Nancy (a pair of maids), and Mr. Thomas (the gardener) bellyache about Reverend Ford's fiery sermon earlier that morning while they shell green peas in preparation for Sunday supper.

Nancy says, "I hate Sundays. Oh, I just hate them." Pollyanna counters by looking on the bright side and pointing out that they get to have roast chicken that day. Nancy glumly asks if Pollyanna is going to start up again with all of her "glad this and glad that." Angie pipes in, asking about all this "glad" business.

Pollyanna explains that it's just a game she plays that she learned from her father. The others in the group keep moaning about why they hate Sundays, but Pollyanna insists this is when they need to play the Glad Game. Angie challenges her by saying, "All right, Miss Smarty Pants. What's so good about Sunday?" Pollyanna thinks for a moment, then replies, "Well, there's always something. You can be glad because . . . because it will be six whole days before Sunday comes around again."[35]

The group chuckles and sends Pollyanna on her way, and she gradually transforms the entire community with her Glad Game and cheerful attitude.

It's a shame, though, how our perception of Pollyanna has changed in 60 years. Being called a "Pollyanna" has become an almost derogatory term to describe someone who's naively optimistic, intentionally blind to unpleasant truths, and woefully out of touch with the harsh realities of life. Today, the *Merriam-Webster Dictionary* defines *Pollyanna* as "a person characterized by irrepressible optimism and a tendency to find good in everything."[36]

Eleanor H. Porter, the author of *Pollyanna*, which became a huge bestseller during the dark days of World War I, even experienced a backlash from reviewers and readers regarding Pollyanna's "unsophisticated reputation" a century ago. "You know, I have been made to suffer from the Pollyanna books," she said in an interview before her death in 1920. "I have been placed often in a false light. People have thought that Pollyanna chirped that she was 'glad' at everything. I have never believed that we ought to deny discomfort and pain and evil; I have merely thought that it is far better to 'greet the unknown with a cheer.'"[37]

Pollyanna's philosophy about finding something to be glad about in any situation is an excellent way to go through life. If there were ever a good time to play the Glad Game, then today would undoubtedly qualify. But no matter what situation or setback you find yourself in, I urge you to ask yourself this question: *What is there to be glad about?*

When it comes to being happy, it's critical to have a healthy brain and train it to look for what makes you happy rather than continually seeking whatever makes you sad, anxious, or afraid.

PRACTICE LOVING-KINDNESS

RESEARCH SHOWS THAT daily prayer and regular attendance at religious services calms stress and reduces the risk of depression, substance abuse, high blood pressure, and cardiovascular disease. Other benefits include a longer life, more happiness, greater overall life satisfaction, better self-control, and increased forgiveness.[38]

In addition, studies have demonstrated that meditation increases dopamine, leading to improved focus and concentration. Meditation is a mental exercise in which you focus your attention on a specific thought, object, or activity for a short period of time. One of my favorite forms is called loving-kindness meditation (LKM), which is intended to develop feelings of goodwill and warmth toward others. It quickly increases positive emotions and decreases negative ones,[39] decreases pain[40] and migraine headaches,[41] reduces symptoms of post-traumatic stress disorder (PTSD)[42] and social prejudice,[43] increases gray matter in the emotional processing areas of the brain,[44] and boosts social connectedness.[45] Here's how to do it:

Sit in a comfortable and relaxed position and close your eyes. Take two or three deep breaths, taking twice as long to exhale. Let any worries or concerns drift away and feel your breath moving through the area around your heart. As you sit, quietly or silently repeat the following or similar phrases:

May I be safe and secure.
May I be healthy and strong.
May I be happy and purposeful.
May I be at peace.

Let the intentions expressed in these phrases sink in as you repeat them. Allow the feelings to grow deeper. After a few repetitions, direct the phrases to someone you feel grateful for or someone who has helped you:

> May you be safe and secure.
> May you be healthy and strong.
> May you be happy and purposeful.
> May you be at peace.

Next visualize someone you feel neutral about. Choose among people you neither like nor dislike and repeat the phrases. Then visualize someone you don't like or with whom you are having a hard time. Kids who are being teased or bullied at school often feel quite empowered when they send love to the people who are making them miserable. Finally, direct the phrases toward everyone universally: "May all beings be safe and secure." You can do this for a few minutes or longer; it's up to you.

THE POWER OF GRATITUDE

ODDS ARE, when most people reflect back on 2020, "grateful" won't top their list of emotions. And yet, that same year, behavioral scientist Steve Maraboli, the author of *Unapologetically You*, published a gratitude journal called *If You Want to Find Happiness, Find Gratitude*.[46] And why not? When we express gratitude, we feel more positive, as does the person we're recognizing.

That's because gratitude directs your attention to positive feelings and away from negative ones. Dr. Hans Selye, considered one of the pioneers of stress research, wrote, "Nothing erases unpleasant thoughts more effectively than conscious concentration on pleasant ones."[47] If I could bottle gratitude and appreciation, I would. The benefits far outweigh most of the medications I prescribe, without any side effects.

In fact, a wealth of research suggests that a daily practice of gratitude, as simple as writing down several things you're grateful for every day, can improve your happiness, mood, self-esteem, resilience, health, looks, productivity, relationships, personality, career, and longevity. Also, when we express our gratitude to others, we strengthen our relationships with them. Unfortunately, sometimes our thank-yous are said so casually or quickly that they are practically meaningless.

To this end, the "father of positivity psychology," Dr. Martin Seligman, came up with a method for expressing gratitude in a thoughtful, purposeful manner. It's called "The Gratitude Visit." This is how he described it:

> Close your eyes. Call up the face of
> someone still alive who years ago
> did something or said something
> that changed your life for the better.
> Someone who you never properly

thanked; someone you could meet face-to-face next week. Got a face? . . .

Your task is to write a letter of gratitude to this individual and deliver it in person. The letter should be concrete and about three hundred words: be specific about what she did for you and how it affected your life. Let her know what you are doing now and mention how you often remember what she did. Make it sing!

Once you have written the testimonial, call the person and tell her you'd like to visit her, but be vague about the purpose of the meeting; this exercise is much more fun when it is a surprise. When you meet her, take your time reading your letter.[48]

Dr. Seligman says that if you're able to read this testimonial in person, be prepared: You'll set off some waterworks. Everyone weeps when a gratitude letter is read. But it works! When Dr. Seligman tested those who participated in a gratitude letter one week, one month, and three months later, they were both happier and less depressed. So, what are you waiting for? Get writing!

LIVE IN THE MOMENT

WE'VE ALL HEARD STOCK phrases like "Live in the here and now" or "Make the most of each day," but research shows that happy people live more fully in the moment than those who are unhappy. A pair of Harvard researchers put this concept to the test when they created an app to analyze people's minute-by-minute thoughts, feelings, and actions.[49] What they discovered is that people tend to think about what is *not* happening almost as much as they think about what *is* happening in the current moment—and this typically makes them unhappy. Conversely, happy people who focus on the present are not preoccupied with past hurts, stressed by regret, or wrapped up in what might happen in the future. Instead, their attention is focused on the present moment, meaning they are aware and mindful of what is happening right now.

Being present-minded is critical to health and happiness. It will ground you and ensure you remain connected to the world around you. This doesn't mean you empty your mind of all thoughts, but your attention is focused on what you're doing, who you're with, and what you're experiencing.

I happened to read the book *The Power of Now*, written by Eckhart Tolle, after I had lost someone important to me and I was grieving. The pain caused me to hunt through past memories, which filled me with regret, anxiety, and chest pain. My gut was not cooperating, and I was miserable.

The most important concept I took from *The Power of Now* was that my thoughts were causing me to suffer as I allowed repetitive thoughts to steal my vital energy. If I wasn't mentally preparing myself for something that would happen in the future, then I was getting lost in the past. But the more I lived in the present moment, the more I felt free from the emotional pain of the past and the worries about the future.

Present-moment thinking is important even during hard times. While we want to get away from or escape pain, we must go *into* the pain. In my book *Your Brain Is Always Listening*, I wrote about the importance of allowing grief to wash over you and to let your tears flow in times of loss.[50] When we acknowledge and go into our pain, it starts to dissipate. By being present and mindful of where we are, we are more apt to feel happy and secure, better handle pain, reduce the impact of stress on our health, and better cope with challenging emotions.[51]

Here's one thing I've done to focus my mind on the present moment. On several consecutive occasions, each time I sat down in my car, I'd feel the steering wheel before I turned on the engine. I would grip the wheel, noting my hand position and the molded material around the rim. Spending a good 20 or 30 seconds on this before driving off was a slowing-life-down exercise that allowed me to "anchor" myself to the present moment. By observing my hands and observing my breathing, I connected my body and mind in the here and now.

Who doesn't need a reminder to grip a steering wheel or smell the roses as we rush through life? When we choose to savor the world around us—from breathing in the comforting smell of fresh laundry coming out of the dryer to slowly enjoying the intricate tastes of food—we refresh our sensory experiences.

Part of living in the present means not worrying about the future, which will kill your happiness every day of the week and twice on Sunday. Worrying may be second nature to many, but most of us are not aware of how much we dwell on fearful thoughts. Research shows that happy people worry far less often than unhappy people do.[52] This insight isn't new, however. In fact, there's a wonderful passage on this concept in the Bible:

> Therefore I tell you, do not worry about your life, what you will eat or drink; or about your body, what you will wear. Is not life more than food, and the body

more than clothes? Look at the birds of
the air; they do not sow or reap or store
away in barns, and yet your heavenly
Father feeds them. Are you not much
more valuable than they? Can any one
of you by worrying add a single hour
to your life?

MATTHEW 6:25-27

ACCENTUATE
THE POSITIVE

TWO THOUSAND YEARS AGO, Paul told the Philippians to "fix your thoughts on what is true, and honorable, and right, and pure, and lovely, and admirable. Think about things that are excellent and worthy of praise" (Philippians 4:8, NLT). And he was right! There is tremendous value in focusing on what's right rather than what is wrong—especially when it comes to thinking about yourself!

Focusing on your strengths rather than your weaknesses is *essential* to living a happy, healthy life. In fact, a 2005 study demonstrated that strength-based interventions boosted happiness and reduced depressive symptoms after just a month. However, it's critical that you actually *use* the identified strengths. Simply talking about them doesn't yield the same benefits.[53]

Let's try a simple exercise. On the lines below, write out five things you're good at (and if you aren't sure, ask your friends what they think you do particularly well):

    1. _____

    2. _____

    3. _____

    4. _____

    5. _____

Now, think of ways to use those attributes in your everyday life. For instance, you may have grown up in a bilingual home and have a proficiency in another language. Could you be putting that skill to better use in your career? The same goes for computer expertise, an ability to cook, or an ability to lead teams. Your personal skills can become your signature strengths.

Granted, when focusing on your strengths, it is critical to have realistic expectations and aspirations. It's interesting how, from a young age, we hear the myth that we can become anything we want to be, even the president of the United States, so we move into our adult years with lofty expectations, but if we learned anything from the pandemic, it's that we can't be sure of *anything* these days.

You will increase your happiness if you scrap or reduce any unrealistic expectations. Chances are, you're not going to have the perfect career, the perfect spouse, or the perfect kids. In fact, seeking perfection is a recipe for unhappiness because you will always be disappointed. Set expectations that make sense to the current situation you find yourself in. And match those expectations with what you've learned about yourself through a strengths-based assessment.

Likewise, focus on your accomplishments. What have you achieved? When I asked one of my patients this question, he answered with "I can't keep a relationship." He had been married 11 times. We then reframed the situation to show him that he was very good at starting relationships and getting women to fall in love with him and began to work on ways he could make the relationships last. In other words, instead of wallowing in what had gone wrong, we noticed what was right and then focused on what could be improved.

So write down those accomplishments and strengths and keep them somewhere you can see them whenever you're feeling down or "less than." It will help you focus on the good, and that will make you happier.

ELIMINATE THE NEGATIVE

YOU KNOW THAT OLD ADAGE "You are what you eat"? Well, there's a lot of truth to that. In fact, scientists are increasingly recognizing that food sensitivities can get you down. Many of the patients we see at Amen Clinics have undetected subtle food allergies that contribute to depression, anxiety, bipolar disorder, fatigue, brain fog, slowed thinking, irritability, agitation, aggression, ADD/ADHD, dementia, and a host of other issues that make people unhappy. What makes these under-the-radar allergies so tricky to identify is that they often don't trigger immediate reactions. In many cases, it can take several days for symptoms to arise. By then, you aren't putting it together that the corn in a seemingly "healthy" salad you ate three days ago is linked to your current down-in-the-dumps mood.

One of the most powerful strategies we use with our patients at Amen Clinics—especially people who have not responded to traditional treatment—is called an elimination diet. This involves ditching the following common allergenic foods—sugar, artificial sweeteners, gluten, soy, corn, dairy, and food additives and dyes—for one month. Seem a little extreme? Well, consider how some of your favorite everyday foods can zap your zest for life:

- **Sugar:** Scheming food manufacturers may try to convince you that the sweet stuff delivers happiness, but it's actually a mood killer. All forms of sugar—even natural honey or maple syrup—cause blood sugar levels to spike and then crash. This negatively impacts mood; increases anxiousness, irritability, and stress; makes you feel fatigued; and causes cravings. Diets that are

too high in sugar also promote inflammation, which is associated with depression
and other issues that make you unhappy.

- **Artificial sweeteners:** Do you think artificial sweeteners are giving you a quick
boost of happiness without the downsides
of sugar? Wrong! Aspartame (NutraSweet,
Equal) has been linked to depression,
anxiety, irritable moods, and insomnia, as
well as a host of other neurophysiological
issues.[54] Artificial sweeteners—including
aspartame, saccharin (Sweet'N Low), and
sucralose (Splenda)—can also lead to high
insulin levels, which are associated with a
higher risk for depression in addition to
Alzheimer's disease and a variety of physical ailments.

- **Gluten:** When I first started talking to my
patients about gluten sensitivity and how
it can negatively impact mood and overall
sense of well-being, most of them had never
heard the word before. These days, "gluten-
free" has become a ubiquitous marketing

buzzword. Even so, gluten continues to be found in breads, cereals, granola, tortillas, and pasta, and it is pumped into foods like barbecue sauce, soy sauce, salad dressings, soups, processed meats, and veggie burgers. This is bad news for the one percent of the US population who have celiac disease, an autoimmune disease in which eating gluten causes damage to the small intestine, and it's also a concern for the estimated 6 percent (almost 20 million) of Americans who have gluten sensitivity.[55]

What do gluten sensitivity and celiac disease have to do with happiness? Research has linked them to depression, anxiety disorders, mood disorders, ADD/ADHD, and other issues that rob you of joy.[56] The good news is that going gluten-free has been found to decrease symptoms of depression, ADD/ADHD, and more. In fact, a 2018 review of 13 studies on gluten and mood symptoms involving 1,139 participants found that eliminating gluten from the diet significantly improved depressive symptoms.[57] The researchers suggested that nixing gluten from the diet may be an effective treatment strategy for mood disorders.

- **Soy:** Head to the grocery store, and you will find the shelves lined with soy-based products—milk alternatives, tofu, tempeh, and edamame, for example. But soy, which is a protein derived from soybeans, is also found in dozens of other food products, such as canned soup, canned tuna, baked goods, cereals, processed meats, protein bars, energy snacks, sauces, and even baby formula. This is problematic because soy contains components that can drain your glass-half-full outlook on life and turn it into a glass-half-empty view. Some of the happiness-robbing compounds in soy include high levels of inflammation-causing omega-6 fatty acids, as well as lectins, which are carbohydrate-binding proteins that can also be toxic. As you have seen, inflammation is linked to depression.

- **Corn:** News flash! Corn is not a vegetable; it is a grain. And its fatty acid profile—high in omega-6 and very low in omega-3—ranks among the worst of all grains. This makes it a sad food that can trigger inflammation and bad moods.

- **Dairy:** The scientific jury is still out on whether there is a connection between dairy consumption and mood issues.[58] However, in my practice, I have seen many patients whose symptoms of depression and anxiety worsen when they eat dairy products and who feel better when they cut them out of their diet. Plus, most dairy cows are raised with hormones and antibiotics.

- **Food additives and dyes:** Artificial dyes, preservatives, flavoring, and other additives have been associated with mood disorders as well as other issues. You may not realize that these culprits might be sucking the happiness out of you because these ingredients hide in so many common food products. Over 10,000 food additives are allowed in the US food supply.[59] And our consumption of artificial food dyes has increased fivefold, according to a 2010 article by the Center for Science in the Public Interest.[60] If you want to be happier, it's worth temporarily eliminating these from your diet. Here's why: Studies on monosodium glutamate (MSG) show that it can trigger depressive and anxious symptoms, among other disturbances.[61] The evidence about Red Dye 40 is even more alarming.[62]

After eliminating these foods for one month, notice how you are feeling. Do you feel more upbeat? Calmer? Less tense? More emotionally stable? More energized? More alert? If so, chances are that one or more of these foods has been causing problems for you.

To find out which food is the culprit, reintroduce each of them to your diet one at a time every three to four days. Eat the reintroduced food at least two to three times a day for three days to see if you notice any physical or psychological reactions. Physical reactions may include headaches, aches and pains, congestion, skin changes, and changes in digestion or bowel functioning. Psychological reactions can include:

Depression
Anxiousness
Anger
Suicidal thoughts
Brain fog
Forgetfulness
Fatigue

If you notice an issue immediately after consumption, stop eating that food at once. If you notice a reaction over the next few days, eliminate that food for 90 days to give your immune system a chance to calm down and your gut a chance to heal. You may want to eliminate that food forever.

But believe me, the end result will be worth it!

JUST BREATHE

CONTRARY TO WHAT MANY PEOPLE might think, *some* anxiety is actually a good thing. When kept in balance, anxiety keeps you safe because your brain is doing its part to protect you from making silly or tragic mistakes. When you have a healthy level of stress before a major test or an important assignment, you're engaged and primed to perform at your highest level. When you're mentally prepared, you understand the parameters and boundaries of the project, which lowers anxiety levels and allows you to perform at your best.

Dr. Daniel Emina, a wonderful psychiatrist who works with me at Amen Clinics, says, "We actually need anxiety. Everybody thinks that anxiety is a bad thing, but you're not supposed to try to completely avoid anxiety. You're supposed to see it as your brain trying to tell you something."

Anxiety is your brain warning you of potential danger. It may be reminding you of something you did that caused you to be injured physically or to be hurt emotionally. Simply put, anxiety is your brain's way of telling you, *Don't make that mistake again!* And that's a good thing!

Dr. Emina says, "I actually get concerned when people go too low in anxiety. Some people will try to get themselves to go really low in anxiety, whether it's with prescribed meds or with nonprescribed options like weed or alcohol. But if you dip your anxiety too low, you will eventually impact your motivation."

The goal should be to strive for a healthy amount of anxiety—enough to motivate you to get things done but not so much that fears and worries prevent you from feeling happy.

Of course, at some point, almost all of us succumb to anxiety attacks—sudden episodes of intense fear based on perceived threats rather than imminent danger. To calm their nerves, some people turn to alcohol, marijuana, or other substances. But there are other, healthier ways to soothe stress and anxiety. In fact, you can get control of your symptoms by following a simple four-step panic plan that I've taught to hundreds of patients.

Step 1: Don't forget to breathe. When anxiety threatens to swallow you, your breathing becomes shallow, rapid, and erratic. Since the brain is the most metabolically active organ in the body, any mental state that lowers the inflow of oxygen will trigger more fear and panic. Stop this downward spiral in its tracks by being mindful that it's happening and taking slow, deep breaths to boost oxygen levels in your brain. The influx of fresh molecules of oxygen will help you regain control over how you feel.

How do you practice deep breathing? By learning how to breathe from your diaphragm, an area of the body that tends to "clench up" when you're anxious. To practice breathing from your diaphragm, try doing this:

Lie on your back and place a small book on
your belly.

As you take 3–4 seconds to slowly inhale
air through your nose, watch the book
rise. Hold your breath at the top of your
inhalation for a second.

When you exhale for 6–8 seconds, watch
the book go down. Then hold your
breath for a second before inhaling again.

Repeat 10 times and notice how relaxed
you feel.

**Step 2: Don't flee even though everything
within you says, "Run!"** When anxiety feels like
it's wrapping you in a bear hug, resist the tempta-
tion to flee for the hills. Do not ignore whatever
is causing your anxiety. Leaving the situation,
unless it is dangerous or life-threatening, allows
the anxiety to control you.

Step 3: Write down your thoughts. Too often in
panicked situations, our thoughts are distorted
and need to be challenged. Pay attention to the
automatic negative thoughts, being sure to write
down or record as many as you can. If you can

show them to a therapist, great, but if not, take a closer look at what you've written. Can any of them be rewritten so that they are a more realistic version of the same thought?

Step 4: Consider a simple supplement, such as GABA or magnesium. Panic attacks often come from overactive anxiety centers, and these supplements can calm them down quickly.

So the next time you find yourself feeling a little anxious, remember—it can be a good thing! Pay attention to what your brain is telling you, and if you start to feel like you're losing control . . . just breathe.

IT'S ALL RELATIVE

RELATIONSHIPS CAN BRING OUT the best in us, or they can make us feel miserable. Positive connections make us feel loved, secure, and content, while troubled relationships drive anxiety, stress, and unhappiness. In fact, a wealth of research points to healthy relationships as the greatest predictor of a happy life.

The good news is, I have a brain-based blueprint for creating more blissful connections with the important people in your life. These clinically proven strategies are rooted in interpersonal psychotherapy, a field that has been shown to decrease depression, anxiety, and stress while elevating marital satisfaction.

To help my patients remember these foundational relationship habits, I use the acronym RELATING:

Responsibility
Empathy
Listening (and good communication
    skills)
Assertiveness (appropriate)
Time
Inquiry (and correcting negative thoughts)
Noticing what you like more than what
    you don't
Grace and forgiveness

R Is for Responsibility

When you accept that it is your moral obligation to be happy for the others in your life, then you are more motivated to work on your relationships to make them stronger. Taking responsibility in your relationships is not about taking the blame for everything or pretending everything is wonderful. It is your ability to respond to whatever is happening in your relationships and taking ownership for finding positive solutions for any existing issues.

To put this concept into action, take a sheet of paper and answer the following three questions so you can start taking more responsibility in your closest relationships.

1. What is the smallest thing I can do today to improve my relationship?

2. When is the last time I blamed my partner, family member, or friend for something, and how did I contribute to the problem? How could I have handled the situation differently?

3. What can I do today to enhance my mood to have a more positive influence on the other person?

E Is for Empathy

Empathy is the human ability to feel what others feel. This concept is based on mirror neurons in the brain, which were discovered by a trio of

Italian neuroscientists in the late nineties. These neurons help us "read" other people's minds and tend to mimic certain actions—like yawning when we see someone else yawn or laughing when someone else starts chuckling.

How can you fire up those mirror neurons and have more empathy for a loved one?

- **Know your loved one's brain type.** Encourage your loved one to take the brain type quiz (brainhealthassessment.com) so you can develop a better understanding of how their brain works.

- **Write down what makes your loved one happy.** Do they love spontaneity, going out with friends, routine, or romantic dinners at home? Look at your list often to remind yourself of what makes them happy.

- **Write down what makes your loved one unhappy.** What are the things that make them irritated, nervous, sad, or stressed? When you are aware of what triggers them, you are less likely to push those buttons.

- **Make an effort to look at things from your partner's point of view.** Before you say or do something, filter it through their lens. And if you're having an argument, listen to their side and take a moment before responding to really try to understand where they're coming from.

- **Mirror your partner.** Watch their body language and adopt a similar stance. Are they leaning forward, gazing into your eyes, or snuggling you? When you mirror their actions, you create a bond.

L Is for Listening (and Good Communication Skills)

Good communication is essential for happy relationships. On the flip side, poor communication can sabotage relationships, even when two people love each other. As a psychiatrist, I have witnessed some really bad listening habits, including:

- Focusing on what you want to say next rather than listening
- Interrupting

- Lack of feedback (verbal or nonverbal)
- Getting distracted
- Lack of eye contact
- Daydreaming
- Rushing the person who is talking
- Finishing the speaker's thoughts

Whenever I notice these traits in the couples I counsel, I encourage them to engage in active listening, which is a technique that marriage counselors are taught to enhance communication. Active listening helps couples build trust, strengthen connections, feel seen and heard, and truly understand each other.

Here are seven strategies to put active listening into practice:

1. **Give feedback to show you are listening:** Smile, nod silently, lean in, or say, "I see," "I understand," "Uh-huh," or "Hmmm."

2. **Allow for periods of silence:** Rather than filling up every second when the other person stops talking, be patient and let them take their time.

3. **Repeat back what has been said:** For example, say, "To make sure I understand, you said . . ." or "So are you saying that . . . ?"

4. **Be neutral and nonjudgmental:** Wait until they are done speaking before giving your opinion.

5. **Ask for clarification:** For example, "To clarify, is this what you mean?"

6. **Ask open-ended questions:** Allow the speaker to expand on their thoughts.

7. **Recap the conversation:** After you have finished, go over a summary of what was discussed.

A Is for Assertiveness (Appropriate)

Being assertive means expressing your thoughts and feelings in a firm yet reasonable way, not allowing others to emotionally run over you, and not saying yes when that's not what you mean.

Here are five simple rules to help you assert yourself in a healthy manner:

1. **Do not give in to the anger of others just because it makes you uncomfortable.** People who experience anxiousness or nervousness are more likely to agree with someone simply to avoid conflict. This strategy often backfires because it teaches the other person that they can bully you to get their way. When someone's anger makes you uncomfortable, take a time-out before responding to their requests or demands. Ideally, wait until they have calmed down—and your anxiety has subsided—before asserting yourself.

2. **Say what you mean, and stick up for what you believe is right.** Some people are hesitant to speak up because they fear they may offend others or their ideas won't be well-received. Practice speaking up and sharing your opinions. You may be surprised to find that others respond more positively to you when you say what's on your mind.

3. **Maintain self-control.** Being angry, mean, or rude is not being assertive. When you feel compelled to verbally let loose on someone,

picture a big STOP sign in your mind, then take a couple of deep breaths, counting to three or four on the inhale and six to eight on the exhale.

4. **Be firm and kind, if possible.** Being firm is an essential part of assertiveness, but kindness also comes into play. When you take a firm stance, it teaches others how to treat you with respect and helps you respect yourself.

5. **Be assertive only when it is necessary.** Most everyday interactions don't require assertiveness. Practice letting go of the little things that aren't that important, but don't be afraid to stand up for yourself in times when it is necessary, such as when someone is trying to take advantage of you, when asking for a deserved promotion at work, or when you need to set boundaries with family members.

T Is for Time

For healthy relationships, you have to invest in what I call special time. During the pandemic, people were spending more time together at home, but it wasn't necessarily quality time. You may have both been working at home together, helping the kids with online learning, or bingeing Netflix but not really connecting on a deep level. What you need to do is carve out time when you can focus on each other. Here are some tips to help you make the most of special time with a loved one:

- **Make a date.** Just like you schedule meeting time at work, put your dates in your calendar. Not only does this help you remember to take this time, but it also enhances its importance in your mind.

- **Go outside.** Getting out of the house, where there are so many distractions—the laundry, the internet, the furniture that needs repairing—can help you focus on each other.

- **Be present.** Keep your mind in the moment rather than thinking about something that happened yesterday or worrying about what might happen in the future.

- **Turn off your cell phones.** To help you stay in tune with each other, take a break from your devices.

- **Do something you both enjoy.** Love hiking? Bowling? Playing Ping-Pong (my personal favorite)? Adding physical activity to your time together encourages the release of the chemicals of happiness that can strengthen your time together.

- **Make time to get romantic (for those in committed relationships).** Sexual intimacy is critical for couples and releases several neurochemicals that promote happiness and bonding. If you have hectic schedules, planning for romance can keep your relationship strong.

I Is for Inquiry (and Correcting Negative Thoughts)

Some people are so wrapped up in their negative thinking patterns that they sabotage their relationships without realizing it. Whenever you have a distressing thought about your relationship, write it down and ask yourself if it is true. Equally important is asking your loved one to explain what they really mean whenever they say something that you interpret in a negative way. Chances are, they didn't mean it that way at all. The next time you have unhappy thoughts about your relationship or you are hurt or angered by something your significant other said, start inquiring.

- Write down your negative thought.
- Ask yourself if it is true.
- Ask your significant other what they meant by what they said. (Use active listening to help you avoid miscommunications.)
- Let them know how you initially interpreted their comment.
- Work together to find a solution to help avoid those miscues in the future.

N Is for Noticing What You Like More Than What You Don't

Have you ever gone out with one of those cringe-worthy couples who bicker incessantly? It can be painful to watch. And it is a sign of an unhappy relationship.

Ultimately, pointing out what your loved one is doing wrong is a de-motivator that drives a wedge between you. Even if you do notice something you don't like about your significant other, family member, or close friend, *you don't have to say it!* We all have weird, crazy, stupid, sexual, violent thoughts that nobody should ever hear. Saying them out loud doesn't help anything.

When you have unkind or critical thoughts, filter them through the question "Does it fit?" There's no rule that you have to say everything you think. Process it, then ask yourself if it fits with your goals for your relationship. Does it get you what you want from your relationship? Assuming you want a kind, caring, loving, supportive, passionate relationship, pointing out your loved one's flaws and shortcomings does not help you achieve that.

What does help you achieve a more loving relationship? Researchers have been looking for the answer to that question for decades. Much of the science points to positive reinforcement as a gateway to a more blissful union. Look at foundational research on happy couples and unhappy couples: The scientists found that distressed married couples were more likely to forego rewarding their partner's loving behaviors in favor of punishing their spouse for bad behavior—criticizing them, interrupting them, complaining, or turning away from them.[63] This pattern of ignoring the good and punishing the bad fueled discord and created an unhappy marriage—it can do the same in any close relationship.

A wealth of research reveals that noticing loving behaviors and rewarding them leads to even more positive behavior.[64] This is called positive reinforcement, and decades of science show it works. For example, married couples who give each other *five times* more positive comments than negative ones are *significantly less likely to get divorced.*[65] The same concept applies to business relationships, where workers who exchange five times more positive comments than negative ones are significantly more likely to be high performing.[66] In this study, the lowest-performing business teams had a higher rate of negativity. Be aware that you can have too much of a good thing. When the ratio of positive comments to negative ones rises beyond nine to one, the effect backfires.

To get started with this strategy, don't expect to be noticing grand gestures like a bouquet of roses, a surprise gift, or a romantic getaway. Look for the micro-moments of loving behavior, the little everyday things that say "I love you," such as:

- When they make dinner for the kids
- When they get your favorite food from the grocery store
- When they fill up your gas tank
- When they compliment your new haircut
- When they wear that shirt you gave them for their birthday
- When they make your morning smoothie so you can sleep in a few minutes
- When they organize a family fun night as a surprise for you

G Is for Grace and Forgiveness

Do you hold grudges or keep reminding your significant other or a family member of past mistakes or transgressions? Do you keep having the same arguments over and over? This is a serious sign of trouble that can sabotage relationships and feed unhappiness. Scientists have found that a lack of forgiveness is associated with increased stress and negative impacts on mental health and physical well-being—all things that suck the happiness out of you.[67]

By contrast, learning to give grace and forgiveness plays an instrumental role in helping a relationship flourish, and it can be powerfully healing. In fact, findings in the *Journal of Happiness Studies* show that forgiveness can make you happier, both in the moment and on a deep-down level.[68] Other studies have linked forgiveness with decreases in depression, anxiety, and other mental health disorders, in addition to fewer physical health problems and reduced mortality rates.[69]

Whenever I talk to my patients about this important topic, I tell them about the REACH forgiveness method, which was developed by psychologist Everett Worthington of Virginia Commonwealth University.[70] REACH stands for:

- **R**ecall the hurt. Try to think about the hurt without feeling like a victim and without holding a grudge.

- Empathize. Try to put yourself in the shoes of the person who hurt you and see the situation from their viewpoint. Can you empathize with what they may have been feeling?

- Altruistic gift. Offer your forgiveness as a gift to the person who caused you pain. If you're having trouble with this step, think of someone who forgave you for something you did and remember how good it made you feel.

- Commit to the forgiveness. Rather than simply thinking about forgiving someone, make it more concrete by writing it down or making a public statement about it.

- Hold on to the forgiveness. If you come in contact with the person who hurt you, you may feel a visceral reaction—anxiousness, anger, or fear, for instance—and think this signals a retraction of your forgiveness. Not so. This is simply your body's way of giving you a warning.

Maintaining happy, healthy relationships takes work. None of these principles are a "one-and-done" event. You'll have to do them again and again and again. But the end result is more than worth it!

DON'T WORRY, BE HYGGE

ACCORDING TO THE ANNUAL *World Happiness Report,* Denmark consistently ranks among the top two or three happiest countries in the world. Are the Danes so happy because tuition for education and health care are free or because crime and political corruption in their country is relatively low? Or is it simply Danish *hygge*?[71]

Hygge (pronounced "hoo-ga") can be loosely translated as "cozy contentment" and relates to a subtle but perceptive ambiance or quality of coziness. Appropriate to Denmark's dismal North Sea climate and 17 hours of daily darkness in winter, *hygge* is about hunkering down and getting snug, perhaps in your jammies, when it's dark and cold outside. Wintertime is when the Danes light candles, build wood fires, and bring out the warm blankets and fuzzy slippers. To show you how much *hygge* is part of the Danish mindset, it's the root of three everyday words:

- *hyggekrog*, or reading nooks
- *hyggebukser*, or comfortable pants
- *hyggesokker*, or woolen socks

Danes like to plan "*hyggelig* evenings" that involve cooking together, gathering around the table for a hearty meal, and then clearing the plates and silverware and bringing out board games. While one can curl up by herself when rain is pelting the roof and binge-watch a TV series, *hygge* is heightened by gathering casually with friends, perhaps in a cozy cabin nestled in the woods, surrounded by snowdrifts.

Hygge helps people appreciate the things that matter most in life. The word originates from the 16th-century Norwegian term *hugga*, which means to comfort or console. It's where we get the word *hug*.

A *hygge* craze took root around 2016 here in the US, spawned by nearly two dozen books about getting in touch with your inner Dane and "taking pleasure in the presence of gentle, soothing things," like a cup of tea and a weighted blanket, said Helen Russell, a British journalist who wrote *The Year of Living Danishly*.[72]

The most well-known printed work is *The Little Book of Hygge* by Meik Wiking, which was released in the US in 2017 after being a big hit in England, where *Oxford Dictionaries* named *hygge* one of its top 10 new words for that year. Reviewers favorably compared the book to Marie Kondo's *The Life-Changing Magic of Tidying Up*. From Maine to Malta to Mauritius, *hygge* spurred a worldwide run on pillar candles and fuzzy blankets.

Wiking shared a typical story about *hygge* when he hung out in a woodsy cabin with friends on Christmas Day. After a long walk through the snow, everyone returned to the rustic hut, where they gathered around a roaring fireplace, wearing thick sweaters and woolen socks, enjoying mulled wine. At the same time, they watched the crackling fire and reminisced about Christmases past. One of Wiking's friends, caught up in the moment, said, "Could this be any more *hygge*?" Everyone nodded in agreement until one woman said: "Yes, if a storm were raging outside."[73]

This reminds me of a joke we have in Newport Beach about Christmas Day: "Let's turn on the air conditioning so we can light a fire." Fortunately, *hygge* is not reserved for Old Man Winter and 10-foot-high piles of snow. Experience *hygge* wherever you are any time of the year.

Here are five ways you can feel happier with *hygge*:

1. Light several candles in the house. Eating dinner by candlelight adds a layer of warm personality and different luminescence to your dining table. Try to use a good mixture of nontoxic scented and unscented candles.

2. Drink warm, indulgent beverages, like hot chocolate. I love hot chocolate, but the traditional form of this sweet treat does not

love me back. Typical hot chocolate is full of sugar, bad fats, and low-quality chocolate—yuck! I decided to do a quick recipe rehab for a brain-healthy version that tastes just as good as—or even better than—the stuff you buy in the store. And it makes you feel good too.

Here's how I make it: I start with organic raw cocoa powder that has no sugar. Real cocoa is a superfood and a powerful anti-oxidant that acts as a natural mood booster. I use about 1 teaspoon of cocoa and add it to about 16 ounces of warm almond milk that is organic, unsweetened, and vanilla fla-vored. Next, I add a few drops of chocolate-flavored stevia and stir it really well. Then, for the pièce de résistance, I use almond milk whipped cream that only has one gram of sugar. It's so delicious and it puts me in a great mood in the evening right before bed-time. What a happy way to end the day!

3. Curl up on the couch with a good book and your shoes off. Put the electronic devices away.

4. Take a walk in nature, away from crowds, through local mountains, along a lakeshore, or on the beach.

5. Invite friends over for a nice dinner. Dinner parties were in rare supply during the pandemic. Get back in the habit of gathering with friends again. Share the cooking responsibilities and experience *hygge*.

So what are you waiting for? Get *hygge*!

GET HAPPY THE NOR WAY!

ANOTHER SCANDINAVIAN COUNTRY, Norway, has its own twist on *hygge*. The Norwegians have a national expression called *friluftsliv* (pronounced "free-loofts-liv"), which means committing to celebrate time outdoors, no matter how bleak the weather forecast is. No huddling around a dazzling fire in jammies and slippers for the Norwegians, who believe that spending time outside in the elements can provide a powerful reset for their mental health. Where *hygge* is about finding comfort indoors, *friluftsliv* is about finding it outdoors.

Friluftsliv, coined in 1859 by Norwegian playwright Henrik Ibsen (his most famous work is *A Doll's House*), means "free air life" but is better translated as "open-air living." *Friluftsliv* suggests a complete understanding of nature's healing effects.

Norwegians will tell you that *friluftsliv* is badly needed because of our collective loss of access to nature. A 2015 study by Stanford researchers found quantifiable evidence that walking in nature yields measurable mental health benefits and may reduce the risk of depression. People who spent 90 minutes walking in a natural area showed decreased activity in the limbic regions of the brain as compared to those participants who strolled through congested urban areas.[74]

"These results suggest that accessible natural areas may be vital for mental health in our rapidly urbanizing world," said study coauthor Gretchen Daily, a senior fellow at the Stanford Woods Institute for the Environment.[75] Presently, half of the world's population lives in an urban setting, which is forecast to rise to almost 70 percent by 2050.[76]

Friluftsliv became a deeper part of Norwegian

culture during the pandemic, when Norwegians looked to the country's love for the outdoors as a respite from enclosed spaces. You have to tip a woolen cap to the Norwegians because the Scandinavian country has some of the worst weather on the planet. A vale of gray clouds covers the country during the short days of winter, and drenching rains are commonplace in summer. But the Norwegians have a chin-up saying that rhymes in their language: *There's no bad weather, only bad clothing.*[77]

So how can we incorporate *friluftsliv*, the idea of reconnecting with nature and having an outdoor lifestyle?

1. Drive outside of town to a nature preserve and walk or hike on a trail that's new to you. Breathe in the fresh air and appreciate the simplicity of the outdoors.

2. Go for a dip. Every January 1, thousands of people participate in Polar Plunges, where participants charge into freezing water that hits like a shot of adrenaline. I can't say I've done one because our local beaches don't have

a formal "polar bear" event. But the idea of a bracing, short dip in chilly water would be one way to start the New Year off in a *friluftsliv* kind of way.

3. Plan a cross-country ski trip. Even if you've never been on cross-country skis, there's not much of a learning curve. A cross-country ski trail can take you deep into the woods and to beautiful vistas you've never seen.

THAT'S THE SPIRIT!

EVEN BEFORE I STARTED medical school, I believed faith and spirituality were important for developing a sense of wholeness. I wanted to learn medicine in the context of my faith, which was why I was thrilled when I got accepted to Oral Roberts University in Tulsa, Oklahoma. At the time, ORU was one of the few Christian medical schools in the nation. We were taught not to see patients as their diseases but rather as whole people in body, mind, relationships, and spirit. Learning to pray with patients, for example, was incredibly powerful.

When I did my psychiatric internship and residency at Walter Reed Army Medical Center in Washington, DC, I taught a course on spirituality and psychiatry to the other residents and hospital staff. In most medical schools, spirituality is nowhere to be found in the psychiatric curriculum. Sigmund Freud, the founder of psychoanalysis, was an atheist who described religion as "a universal obsessional neurosis" and science's "really serious enemy . . . unworthy of belief."[78]

Yet, according to psychiatrist Harold Koenig, director of the Center for Spirituality, Theology and Health at Duke University Medical Center, 89 percent of Americans believe in God, 90 percent pray on a regular basis, and 82 percent acknowledge the need for spiritual growth.[79] Psychiatrists should understand those beliefs, work within their context, and never diminish or dismiss them. They should explore supporting a person's deepest sense of meaning and purpose.

Science is beginning to catch up to the importance of spirituality in people's mental health and well-being. For example, research has shown that attending religious services on a regular basis and daily prayer are associated with many health benefits, including a decreased risk of stress, depression, addiction, hypertension, and heart disease, and an increase in forgiveness, self-control, longevity, happiness, and life satisfaction.[80]

Without faith in our lives, we would be like a four-legged stool that is missing one leg. So how can you foster a closer relationship with God?

1. **Spend time in Scripture:** Knowing God's promises and obeying his commands are essential to a healthy spiritual life. If you think about it, the Scriptures are a road map for how we are to communicate with God and each other. They direct us in how we are supposed to live. If we stray from his Word—if we forget his promises—then just like a driver without GPS, we will get lost. Meditating on God's Word helps us stay the course—*and* it brings us closer to him.

2. **Pray every day:** In Matthew 11:28-29, Jesus encourages us to let go of our burdens and rest in him, and there is no better way to do that than to spend time praying and quietly

meditating on his Word. Not only are meditation and prayer vital to a healthy spiritual life, they are also wonderful stress-management tools. In fact, research has shown that people who pray and meditate regularly have better focus, judgment, and impulse control, which enables them to make more thoughtful and moral decisions.

3. **Practice forgiveness:** Nothing wreaks havoc on your body and soul quite like bitterness and hatred. When you hold on to anger and resentment, the cells in your body are put into a tense state, which damages your immune system and impairs your ability to think and remember things clearly. However, much like love, forgiveness brings healing. When you forgive, you let go of negativity and pain, restoring your body and mind to a healthy state. Think of someone you are struggling to forgive and ask God to help you let go of your anger. You will be amazed by how healing it is!

4. **Find a faith community:** We need other people in our lives to thrive emotionally and

spiritually. If you're looking for new ways to build community, try getting involved with your local church. But don't stop there. Volunteer at a local food pantry, go on a missions trip, or join some friends in a weekly Bible study.

5. **Keep looking up:** Start every day with the phrase "Today is going to be a great day," and following Paul's advice in Philippians 4:8, keep your thoughts fixed on what is true, honorable, right, pure, and lovely.

LOVE—
YOUR SECRET WEAPON

WHEN JESUS TOLD US TO love each other as ourselves, he was giving us good health advice. Research suggests that whenever you feel down, anxious, or angry, it is best to get outside yourself to change your state of mind. In a new study, people who wrote about gratitude activated a part of their brains involved in happiness and altruism.[81]

That said, if you want to feel better, go to the aid of someone who needs help. According to a *New York Times* story, in the 1970s, former First Lady Barbara Bush became so depressed that she sometimes stopped her car on the side of the road for fear that she might deliberately crash the vehicle into a tree or an oncoming car. Mrs. Bush did not seek psychiatric help or medication for her depression, which she blamed on the hormonal changes of menopause and the stress of her husband's job as CIA director. Instead, she said she treated her depression by immersing herself in volunteer work and getting outside herself to help others.[82]

Being loving to strangers—or even to people you know—has the added benefit of making you feel happier, according to two studies. In one study, 86 participants were asked about their life satisfaction and then divided into three groups. The first group was told to do an act of kindness every day for 10 days; the second group was told to do something new every day for 10 days; and the third group was given no instruction. When the 10 days had passed, the groups were retested on life satisfaction. Levels of happiness increased significantly and nearly equally among participants in the groups that had performed acts of kindness or novel activities, while happiness didn't change at all in the group that did neither.[83] Doing something for others for 10 days, especially if you vary the good deeds, is an effective way to make yourself feel better, the study suggests.

In another study, participants were divided into two groups and asked to recall either the last time they spent either $20 or $100 on themselves or the last time they had spent the same amount on someone else. After completing a scale measuring their levels of happiness, all of the participants were provided with a small sum of money and given the option of spending the money on themselves or on another person. The researchers found that study subjects were happier when they were asked to recall a time when they had purchased something for someone else, no matter the price of the gift. What's more, the happier they felt about being generous in the past, the greater the likelihood that they would spend money on someone besides themselves.[84] As the Bible states, "It is more blessed to give than to receive" (Acts 20:35).

Finally, research shows the happiest people are outward facing, focusing more on the people they serve than on themselves.[85]

Even though the prayer attributed to

St. Francis of Assisi was likely not written by him, it still provides a research-based guide to happiness. The next time you feel stressed, consider repeating it or any other similar prayer or meditation, such as the Loving-Kindness Meditation.

PEACE PRAYER OF ST. FRANCIS

Lord, make me an instrument of your peace:
where there is hatred, let me sow love;
where there is injury, pardon;
where there is doubt, faith;
where there is despair, hope;
where there is darkness, light;
where there is sadness, joy.

O divine Master, grant that I may not
     so much seek
to be consoled as to console,
to be understood as to understand,
to be loved as to love.
For it is in giving that we receive,
it is in pardoning that we are pardoned,
and it is in dying that we are born to
     eternal life.
Amen.

By consciously bringing your attention to what you are grateful for, the people who bring you joy, and your own successes, you'll see a decrease in worry, anxiety, anger, and negativity and be on your way to feeling happier.

THE MOST IMPORTANT QUESTION TO ASK YOURSELF

TO TRULY FEEL AND BE YOUR BEST, you need to love and care for the three-pound super-computer between your ears. Yet very few people really care about their brains, likely because they cannot see them. You can see the wrinkles in your skin, the fat around your belly, the flab on your arms, or the graying hair around your temples. But because very few people ever really look at their brains (via imaging studies), many just don't pay attention to them. As a result, they don't care about them, which is why they tend to develop unhealthy habits like drinking too much alcohol, smoking pot, eating low-quality fast food on the run, and not making sleep a priority.

But once you truly love your brain, everything in your life changes because you have a heightened sense of urgency to care for it. Think about it. If you had a $300,000 Ferrari, would you ever pour sugar or salt into the gas tank? Would you run it until it couldn't go anymore without maintenance? Of course not! Well . . . isn't your brain worth so much more? Of course it is! Your brain needs you to love and care for it, or it will never be able to fully take care of you.

So how can you start loving your brain right here and now? It's actually very simple. Whenever you come to a decision point in your day, ask yourself: *Is the decision I'm about to make good for my brain or bad for it?*

For example, let's say you just had a fight with your spouse. Should you

1. respond in anger and tell him or her exactly what's on your mind?

2. have a donut to calm your nerves?

3. grab an apple and a few nuts, and take a walk to calm down and consider what you can do to make the situation better?

Or what if your stock portfolio went down after a stock market sell-off? Should you

1. stay up all night to figure out your next best move?

2. make sure you get seven hours of sleep so you are well rested and can make good decisions about your stocks the next day?

3. smoke a joint to relax?

One more: Pretend your boss just told you she was unhappy with your performance. Should you

1. skip lunch, put your head down, and work harder?

2. complain to your coworkers about how unreasonable your boss is over a beer and nachos after work?

3. take a walk to clear your head, and when you return, ask your boss for feedback on how you can improve?

It's really pretty straightforward if you think about it, isn't it? The bottom line is this: If you make a habit of asking, *Is this decision good for my brain or bad for it?* at the moment of choice, and then make the decision that is in the best interest of the health of your brain, you'll feel happier and be less anxious and more fully equipped to handle whatever challenges come your way!

ABOUT THE AUTHOR

DANIEL G. AMEN, MD, believes that brain health is central to all health and success. When your brain works right, he says, you work right, and when your brain is troubled, you are much more likely to have trouble in your life. His work is dedicated to helping people have better brains and better lives.

Sharecare named him the web's #1 most influential expert and advocate on mental health, and the *Washington Post* called him the most popular psychiatrist in America. His online videos have been viewed more than 150 million times.

Dr. Amen is a physician, board-certified child and adult psychiatrist, award-winning researcher, and 12-time *New York Times* bestselling author. He is the founder and CEO of Amen Clinics in Costa Mesa, Walnut Creek, and Encino, California; Bellevue, Washington; Washington, DC; Atlanta; Chicago; Dallas; New York; Hollywood, FL; and Scottsdale, Arizona.

Amen Clinics has the world's largest database of functional brain scans relating to behavior, with more than 200,000 SPECT scans and more than 10,000 QEEGs on patients from over 150 countries.

Dr. Amen is the lead researcher on the world's largest brain imaging and rehabilitation study on professional football players. His research has not only demonstrated high levels of brain damage in players but also the possibility of significant recovery for many with the principles that underlie his work.

Together with Pastor Rick Warren and Dr. Mark Hyman, Dr. Amen is also one of the chief architects of The Daniel Plan, a program to get the world healthy through religious organizations, which has been done in thousands of churches, mosques, and synagogues.

Dr. Amen is the author or coauthor of more than 80 professional articles, 9 book chapters, and over 40 books, including 18 national bestsellers and 12 *New York Times* bestsellers, including the #1 *New York Times* bestsellers *The Daniel Plan* and the over-one-million-copies-sold, 40-week bestseller *Change Your Brain, Change Your Life*; as well as *The End of Mental Illness*; *Healing ADD*; *Change Your Brain, Change Your Body*; *The Brain Warrior's Way*; *Memory Rescue*; *Your Brain Is Always Listening*; and *You, Happier.*

Dr. Amen's published scientific articles have appeared in the prestigious journals of *Journal of Alzheimer's Disease*, Nature's *Molecular Psychiatry*, *PLOS ONE*, Nature's *Translational Psychiatry*, Nature's *Obesity*, *Journal of Neuropsychiatry and Clinical Neuroscience*, *Minerva Psichiatrica*, *Journal of Neurotrauma*, *American Journal of Psychiatry*, *Nuclear Medicine Communications*, *Neurological Research*, *Journal of the American Academy of Child and Adolescent Psychiatry*, *Primary Psychiatry*, *Military Medicine*, and *General Hospital Psychiatry*.

In January 2016, his team's research on distinguishing PTSD from TBI on over 21,000 SPECT scans was featured as one of the top 100 stories in science by *Discover* magazine. In 2017, his team published a study on over 46,000 scans, showing the difference between male and female brains; and in 2018, his team published a study on how the brain ages based on 62,454 SPECT scans.

Dr. Amen has written, produced, and hosted 17 national public television programs about brain health, which have aired more than 150,000 times across North America. As of March 2023, his latest show is *Change Your Brain Every Day.*

Dr. Amen has appeared in movies, including *Quiet Explosions, After the Last Round,* and *The Crash Reel,* and was a consultant for *Concussion,* starring Will Smith. He appeared in the docuseries *Justin Bieber: Seasons* and has appeared regularly on *The Dr. Oz Show, Dr. Phil,* and *The Doctors.*

He has also spoken for the National Security Agency (NSA), the National Science Foundation (NSF), Harvard's Learning and the Brain Conference, the Department of the Interior, the National Council of Juvenile and Family Court Judges, the Supreme Courts of Ohio, Delaware, and Wyoming, the Canadian and Brazilian Societies of Nuclear Medicine, and large corporations, such as Merrill Lynch, Hitachi, Bayer Pharmaceuticals,

GNC, and many others. In 2016, Dr. Amen gave one of the prestigious Talks at Google.

Dr. Amen's work has been featured in *Newsweek*, *Time*, *Huffington Post*, *ABC World News*, *20/20*, the BBC, *London Telegraph*, *Parade* magazine, the *New York Times*, the *New York Times Magazine*, the *Washington Post*, *MIT Technology*, World Economic Forum, the *Los Angeles Times*, *Men's Health*, Bottom Line, *Vogue*, *Cosmopolitan*, and many others.

In 2010, Dr. Amen founded BrainMD, a fast-growing nutraceutical company dedicated to natural ways to support mental health and brain health.

Dr. Amen is married to Tana and is the father of four children and grandfather to Elias, Emmy, Liam, Louie, and Haven. He is an avid table tennis player.

NOTES

1. Michael Argyle, Peter Hills, and Stephen Wright, "Take the Oxford Happiness Questionnaire," *Guardian*, November 3, 2014, https://www .theguardian.com/lifeandstyle/2014/nov/03 /take-the-oxford-happiness-questionnaire.
2. Nicole Celestine, "The Science of Happiness in Positive Psychology 101," *Happiness & SWB* (blog), January 26, 2017, PositivePsychology.com, last updated August 11, 2022, https://positivepsychology .com/happiness/.
3. Majid Fotuhi, "Can You Grow Your Hippocampus? Yes. Here's How, and Why It Matters," SharpBrains, November 4, 2015, http://sharpbrains.com/blog /2015/11/04/can-you-grow-your-hippocampus-yes -heres-how-and-why-it-matters/.

4. Felice N. Jacka et al., "A Randomized, Controlled Trial of Dietary Improvement for Adults with Major Depression (the 'SMILES' Trial)," *BMC Medicine* 15, no. 1 (January 30, 2017).

5. Shawn Achor and Michelle Gielan, "Consuming Negative News Can Make You Less Effective at Work," *Harvard Business Review*, September 14, 2015, https://hbr.org/2015/09/consuming-negative-news-can-make-you-less-effective-at-work.

6. Jun Sugawara, Takashi Tarumi, and Hirofumi Tanaka, "Effect of Mirthful Laughter on Vascular Function," *American Journal of Cardiology* 106, no. 6 (September 15, 2010): 856–59, https://pubmed.ncbi.nlm.nih.gov/20816128/.

7. Pedro Marques-Vidal and Virginia Milagre, "Are Oral Health Status and Care Associated with Anxiety and Depression? A Study of Portuguese Health Science Students," *Journal of Public Health Dentistry* 66, no. 1 (Winter 2006): 64–66, https://pubmed.ncbi.nlm.nih.gov/16570753/.

8. Nancy L. Sin, Jennifer E. Graham-Engeland, and David M. Almeida, "Daily Positive Events and Inflammation: Findings from the National Study of Daily Experiences," *Brain, Behavior, and Immunity* 43 (January 2015): 130–38, https://www.sciencedirect.com/science/article/abs/pii/S0889159114004073.

9. Meike Bartels, "Genetics of Wellbeing and Its Components Satisfaction with Life, Happiness, and Quality of Life: A Review and Meta-analysis of Heritability Studies," *Behavior Genetics* 45, no. 2 (March 2015): 137–56, https://pubmed.ncbi.nlm.nih.gov/25715755/.

10. Floriana S. Luppino et al., "Overweight, Obesity, and Depression: A Systematic Review and Meta-analysis of Longitudinal Studies," *Archives of General Psychiatry* 67, no. 3 (2010): 220–29, https://pubmed.ncbi.nlm.nih.gov/20194822/.

11. Centers for Disease Control and Prevention, "The Surprising Truth about Prediabetes," last reviewed July 7, 2022, https://www.cdc.gov/diabetes/library/features/truth-about-prediabetes.html.

12. Yaron Steinbuch, "90% of Americans Eat Garbage," *New York Post*, November 17, 2017, https://nypost.com/2017/11/17/90-of-americans-eat-like-garbage/.
    Centers for Disease Control and Prevention, "Only 1 in 10 Adults Get Enough Fruits or Vegetables," November 16, 2017, https://www.cdc.gov/media/releases/2017/p1116-fruit-vegetable-consumption.html.

13. Charles W. Popper, "Single-Micronutrient and Broad-Spectrum Micronutrient Approaches for Treating Mood Disorders in Youth and Adults," *Child and Adolescent Psychiatric Clinics of North America* 23, no. 3 (July 2014): 591–672, https://www.sciencedirect.com/science/article/abs/pii/S1056499314000315?via%3Dihub.

14. Meredith Blampied et al., "Broad Spectrum Micronutrient Formulas for the Treatment of Symptoms of Depression, Stress, and/or Anxiety: A Systematic Review," *Expert Review of Neurotherapeutics* 20, no. 4 (April 2020): 351–71, https://pubmed.ncbi.nlm.nih.gov/32178540/.

15. Allen T. G. Lansdowne and Stephen C. Provost, "Vitamin D3 Enhances Mood in Healthy Subjects during Winter," *Psychopharmacology* 135, no. 4

(February 1998): 319–23, https://link.springer
.com/article/10.1007%2Fs002130050517.

16. Felice N. Jacka et al., "Dietary Patterns and
    Depressive Symptoms over Time: Examining the
    Relationships with Socioeconomic Position, Health
    Behaviours and Cardiovascular Risk," *PLOS ONE* 9,
    no. 1 (January 29, 2014): e87657, https://pubmed
    .ncbi.nlm.nih.gov/24489946/.

    Behnaz Shakersain et al., "Prudent Diet May
    Attenuate the Adverse Effects of Western Diet on
    Cognitive Decline," *Alzheimer's and Dementia* 12,
    no. 2 (February 2016): 100–109, https://alz-journals
    .onlinelibrary.wiley.com/doi/full/10.1016/j.jalz
    .2015.08.002.

    Amber L. Howard et al., "ADHD Is Associated
    with a 'Western' Dietary Pattern in Adolescents,"
    Journal of Attention Disorders 15, no. 5 (2011):
    403–11, https://journals.sagepub.com/doi
    /10.1177/1087054710365990.

    Giovanni Tarantino, Vincenzo Citro, and
    Carmine Finelli, "Hype or Reality: Should Patients
    with Metabolic Syndrome–related NAFLD Be
    on the Hunter-Gatherer (Paleo) Diet to Decrease
    Morbidity?" *Journal of Gastrointestinal and Liver
    Diseases* 24, no. 3 (September 2015): 359–68,
    https://pubmed.ncbi.nlm.nih.gov/26405708/.

17. DeAnn Liska et al., "Narrative Review of Hydration
    and Selected Health Outcomes in the General
    Population," *Nutrients* 11, no. 1 (January 2019):
    70, https://www.ncbi.nlm.nih.gov/pmc/articles
    /PMC6356561/.

18. Shayla Love, "Why You Should Talk to Yourself
    in the Third Person," *Vice*, December 28, 2020,

https://www.vice.com/en/article/k7a3mm/why-you-should-talk-to-yourself-in-the-third-person-inner-monologue.

19. Daniel G. Amen, *Healing ADD from the Inside Out*, rev. ed. (New York: Berkley Books, 2013), chapter 23.

20. Patricia A. Boyle et al., "Effect of a Purpose in Life on Risk of Incident Alzheimer Disease and Mild Cognitive Impairment in Community-Dwelling Older Persons," *Archives of General Psychiatry* 67, no. 3 (March 2010): 304–10, https://www.ncbi.nlm.nih.gov/pmc/articles/PMC2897172/.

21. Aliya Alimujiang et al., "Association between Life Purpose and Mortality among US Adults Older Than 50 Years," *JAMA Network Open* 2, no. 5 (May 3, 2019): e194270, https://pubmed.ncbi.nlm.nih.gov/31125099/.

22. Andrew Steptoe, Angus Deaton, and Arthur A. Stone, "Subjective Wellbeing, Health, and Ageing," *Lancet* 385, no. 9968 (February 14, 2015): 640–48, https://pubmed.ncbi.nlm.nih.gov/25468152/.

23. Anthony L. Burrow and Nicolette Rainone, "How Many *Likes* Did I Get?: Purpose Moderates Links between Positive Social Media Feedback and Self-Esteem," *Journal of Experimental Social Psychology* 69 (March 2017): 232–36, https://www.sciencedirect.com/science/article/abs/pii/S0022103116303377.

24. Elisabeth Kübler-Ross, *Death: The Final Stage of Growth* (New York: Simon & Schuster, 1986), 164. See also Elisabeth Kübler-Ross, *On Death and Dying: What the Dying Have to Teach Doctors, Nurses, Clergy and Their Own Families*, 50th anniversary ed. (New York: Scribner, 2014).

25. Chinese proverb, Goodreads, https://www.goodreads
.com/quotes/7956059-if-you-want-happiness-for-an
-hour-take-a.

26. *The Curious Case of Benjamin Button*, directed by
David Fincher (Hollywood, CA: Paramount, 2008).

27. Elisabeth Sifton, *The Serenity Prayer: Faith and
Politics in Times of Peace and War* (New York:
Norton, 2003), 13.

28. Byron Katie with Stephen Mitchell, *Loving What
Is: Four Questions That Can Change Your Life*
(New York: Harmony Books, 2002), xv–xix.

29. Janelle Ringer, "Laughter: A Fool-Proof Prescription,"
Loma Linda University Health, April 1, 2019, https://
news.llu.edu/research/laughter-fool-proof-prescription.

30. Jennifer Aaker and Naomi Bagdonas, *Humor,
Seriously: Why Humor Is a Secret Weapon in Business
and Life* (New York: Currency, 2021), 43–44.

31. C. Hublin et al., "Heritability and Mortality
Risk of Insomnia-Related Symptoms: A Genetic
Epidemiologic Study in a Population-Based Twin
Cohort," *Sleep* 34, no. 7 (July 1, 2011): 957-64,
https://doi.org/10.5665/SLEEP.1136.

32. Joseph McClendon III, *Get Happy NOW!* (n.p.:
Success, 2012).

33. *Justin Bieber: Seasons* (YouTube Originals, 2020),
episode 9, "Album on the Way," February 17, 2020,
video, 9:51, https://www.youtube.com/watch?v
=pWcI-BeQqls&t=361s.

    Kerry Breen, "What Is Havening? Experts Weigh
In on Justin Bieber's Stress-Relieving Technique,"
TODAY.com, March 3, 2020, https://www.today
.com/health/what-havening-experts-weigh-justin
-bieber-s-stress-relieving-technique-t174747.

34. Havening Techniques, "Havening Touch," https://www.havening.org/about-havening/havening-touch.

35. "Pollyanna—The Glad Game," September 6, 2012, video, 1:47, from *Pollyanna*, directed by David Swift (Burbank, CA: Walt Disney Productions, 1960), https://www.youtube.com/watch?v=1Ihxyf7A1hg.

36. *Merriam-Webster Dictionary*, 11th ed. (2003), s.v. "Pollyanna."

37. Ruth Graham, "How We All Became Pollyannas (and Why We Should Be Glad about It)," *Atlantic*, February 26, 2013, https://www.theatlantic.com /entertainment/archive/2013/02/how-we-all-became -pollyannas-and-why-we-should-be-glad-about-it /273323/.

38. Shanshan Li et al., "Religious Service Attendance and Lower Depression among Women—a Prospective Cohort Study," *Annals of Behavioral Medicine* 50, no. 6 (December 2016): 876–84, https://academic .oup.com/abm/article/50/6/876/4562664.

39. Xianglong Zeng et al., "The Effect of Loving-Kindness Meditation on Positive Emotions: A Meta-Analytic Review," *Frontiers in Psychology* 6 (November 3, 2015): 1693, https://doi.org/10.3389 /fpsyg.2015.01693.

    Barbara L. Fredrickson et al., "Open Hearts Build Lives: Positive Emotions, Induced through Loving-Kindness Meditation, Build Consequential Personal Resources," *Journal of Personality and Social Psychology* 95, no.5 (November 2008): 1045–1062, https://doi.org/10.1037/a0013262.

40. James W. Carson et al., "Loving-Kindness Meditation for Chronic Low Back Pain: Results from a Pilot Trial," *Journal of Holistic Nursing* 23,

no.3 (September 2005): 287–304, https://doi.org
/10.1177/0898010105277651.

41. Makenzie E. Tonelli and Amy B. Wachholtz,
"Meditation-Based Treatment Yielding Immediate
Relief for Meditation-Naïve Migraineurs," *Pain
Management Nursing* 15, no.1 (March 2014): 36–40,
https://doi.org/10.1016/j.pmn.2012.04.002.

42. David J. Kearney et al., "Loving-Kindness
Meditation for Posttraumatic Stress Disorder:
A Pilot Study," *Journal of Traumatic Stress* 26,
no. 4 (August 2013): 426–34, https://doi.org
/10.1002/jts.21832.

43. Alexander J. Stell and Tom Farsides, "Brief Loving-
Kindness Meditation Reduces Racial Bias, Mediated
by Positive Other-Regarding Emotions," *Motivation
and Emotion* 40, no.1 (September 9, 2015): 140–47,
https://doi.org/10.1007/s11031-015-9514-x.

44. Mei-Kei Leung et al., "Increased Gray Matter
Volume in the Right Angular and Posterior
Parahippocampal Gyri in Loving-Kindness
Meditators," *Social Cognitive and Affective
Neuroscience* 8, no. 1 (January 2013): 34–39,
https://doi.org/10.1093/scan/nss076.

45. Bethany E. Kok et al., "How Positive Emotions
Build Physical Health: Perceived Positive Social
Connections Account for the Upward Spiral between
Positive Emotions and Vagal Tone," *Psychological
Science* 24, no. 7 (July 2013): 1123–32, https://doi
.org/10.1177/0956797612470827.

46. Steve Maraboli, *If You Want to Find Happiness, Find
Gratitude* (self-pub., 2020).

47. Hans Selye, *The Stress of Life*, rev. ed. (New York:
McGraw-Hill, 1956, 1976), 418.

48. Martin E. P. Seligman, *Flourish* (New York: Free Press, 2011), 30–31.

49. Matthew A. Killingsworth and Daniel T. Gilbert, "A Wandering Mind Is an Unhappy Mind," *Science* 330, no. 6006 (November 12, 2010): 932, https:// pubmed.ncbi.nlm.nih.gov/21071660/.

50. Daniel G. Amen, *Your Brain Is Always Listening* (Carol Stream, IL: Tyndale, 2021), 63–64.

51. Courtney E. Ackerman, "How to Live in the Present Moment: 35+ Exercises and Tools to Be More Present," PositivePsychology.com, updated July 5, 2022, https://positivepsychology.com/present-moment/.

52. Ackerman, "How to Live in the Present Moment."

53. Cited in Bryant M. Stone and Acacia C. Parks, "Cultivating Subjective Well-Being through Positive Psychological Interventions," in *Handbook of Well-Being*, ed. Ed Diener, Shigehiro Oishi, and Louis Tay (Salt Lake City: DEF Publishers, 2018), https://www.nobascholar.com/chapters /59/download.pdf.

54. Arbind Kumar Choudhary and Yeong Yeh Lee, "Neurophysiological Symptoms and Aspartame: What Is the Connection?" *Nutritional Neuroscience* 21, no. 5 (June 2018): 306–16, https://pubmed.ncbi .nlm.nih.gov/28198207/.

55. Samuel O. Igbinedion et al., "Non-celiac Gluten Sensitivity: All Wheat Attack Is Not Celiac," *World Journal of Gastroenterology* 23, no. 40 (2017): 7201–10, https://www.ncbi.nlm.nih.gov/pmc /articles/PMC5677194/.

56. Jessica R. Jackson et al., "Neurologic and Psychiatric Manifestations of Celiac Disease and Gluten Sensitivity," *Psychiatric Quarterly* 83, no. 1 (March

2012): 91–102, https://www.ncbi.nlm.nih.gov/pmc/articles/PMC3641836/.

57. Eleanor Busby et al., "Mood Disorders and Gluten: It's Not All in Your Mind! A Systematic Review with Meta-Analysis," *Nutrients* 10, no. 11 (November 8, 2018): 1708, https://pubmed.ncbi.nlm.nih.gov/30413036/.

58. Meghan Hockey et al., "Is Dairy Consumption Associated with Depressive Symptoms or Disorders in Adults? A Systematic Review of Observational Studies," *Critical Reviews in Food Science and Nutrition* 60, no. 21 (2020): 3653–68, https://pubmed.ncbi.nlm.nih.gov/31868529/.

59. Pew Charitable Trusts, "Fixing the Oversight of Chemicals Added to Our Food," November 7, 2013, https://www.pewtrusts.org/en/research-and-analysis/reports/2013/11/07/fixing-the-oversight-of-chemicals-added-to-our-food.

60. Center for Science in the Public Interest, "CSPI Says Food Dyes Pose Rainbow of Risks," June 29, 2010, https://cspinet.org/new/201006291.html.

61. Caroline B. Quines et al., "Monosodium Glutamate, a Food Additive, Induces Depressive-like and Anxiogenic-like Behaviors in Young Rats," *Life Sciences* 107, nos. 1–2 (June 27, 2014): 27–31, https://www.sciencedirect.com/science/article/abs/pii/S0024320514004524.

62. Amen Clinics, "Brain Health Guide to Red Dye #40," June 14, 2016, https://www.amenclinics.com/blog/brain-health-guide-red-dye-40/.

63. Gary R. Birchler, Robert L. Weiss, and John P. Vincent, "Multimethod Analysis of Social Reinforcement Exchange between Maritally

Distressed and Nondistressed Spouse and Stranger Dyads," *Journal of Personality and Social Psychology* 31, no. 2 (1975): 349–60, https://psycnet.apa.org/record/1975-11572-001.

John M. Gottman and R. W. Levenson, "Marital Processes Predictive of Later Dissolution: Behavior, Physiology, and Health," *Journal of Personality and Social Psychology* 63, no. 2 (1992): 221–33, https://doi.org/10.1037/0022-3514.63.2.221.

64. Marshall Lev Dermer, "Towards Understanding the Meaning of Affectionate Verbal Behavior; Towards Creating Romantic Loving," *Behavior Analyst Today* 7, no. 4 (2006): 452–80, https://doi.apa.org/fulltext/2010-10811-002.html.

65. Gottman and Levenson, "Marital Processes Predictive of Later Dissolution."

66. Marcial Losada and Emily Heaphy, "The Role of Positivity and Connectivity in the Performance of Business Teams: A Nonlinear Dynamics Model," *American Behavioral Scientist* 47, no. 6 (February 1, 2004): 740–65, https://journals.sagepub.com/doi/10.1177/0002764203260208.

67. Loren Toussaint et al., "Effects of Lifetime Stress Exposure on Mental and Physical Health in Young Adulthood: How Stress Degrades and Forgiveness Protects Health," *Journal of Health Psychology* 21, no. 6 (June 2016): 1004–14, https://pubmed.ncbi.nlm.nih.gov/25139892/.

68. John Maltby, Liza Day, and Louise Barber, "Forgiveness and Happiness. The Differing Contexts of Forgiveness Using the Distinction between Hedonic and Eudaimonic Happiness," *Journal of Happiness*

Studies 6, no. 1 (March 2005): 1–13, https://link
.springer.com/article/10.1007/s10902-004-0924-9.

69. Kirsten Weir, "Forgiveness Can Improve Mental
and Physical Health," *Monitor on Psychology* 48,
no. 1 (January 2017): 30, http://www.apa.org
/monitor/2017/01/ce-corner.aspx.

70. I wrote about the REACH method in *Your Brain Is
Always Listening* (Carol Stream, IL: Tyndale, 2021),
53–54.
    Everett Worthington, "Research," http://www
.evworthington-forgiveness.com/research.

71. Denmark.dk, "Why Are Danish People So Happy?"
https://denmark.dk/people-and-culture/happiness.

72. Quoted in Anna Altman, "The Year of Hygge, the
Danish Obsession with Getting Cozy," *New Yorker*,
December 18, 2016, https://www.newyorker.com
/culture/culture-desk/the-year-of-hygge-the-danish
-obsession-with-getting-cozy.

73. Altman, "The Year of Hygge."

74. Rob Jordan, "Stanford Researchers Find Mental
Health Prescription: Nature," *Stanford News*,
June 30, 2015, https://news.stanford.edu/2015
/06/30/hiking-mental-health-063015/.

75. Jordan, "Stanford Researchers Find Mental Health
Prescription."

76. United Nations Department of Economic and
Social Affairs, "68% of the World Population
Projected to Live in Urban Areas by 2050, Says
UN," May 16, 2018, https://www.un.org
/development/desa/en/news/population/2018
-revision-of-world-urbanization-prospects.html.

77. Jen Rose Smith, "What Is 'Friluftsliv'? How an Idea
of Outdoor Living Could Help Us This Winter,"

National Geographic, September 11, 2020, https://
www.nationalgeographic.com/travel/article/how
-norways-friluftsliv-could-help-us-through-a
-coronavirus-winter.

78. Hans Küng, "Freud and the Problem of God,"
Wilson Quarterly 3, no. 4 (Autumn 1979): 162–71,
https://www.jstor.org/stable/40255732?seq=1.

79. Jeanne McCauley et al., "Spiritual Beliefs and
Barriers among Managed Care Practitioners,"
Journal of Religion and Health 44, no. 2 (Summer
2005): 137–46, https://pubmed.ncbi.nlm.nih
.gov/16021729/.

  Harold G. Koenig, "Religion, Spirituality, and
Health: The Research and Clinical Implications,"
ISRN Psychiatry 2012 (2012): 278730, https://www
.ncbi.nlm.nih.gov/pmc/articles/PMC3671693/.

80. Shanshan Li et al., "Religious Service Attendance and
Lower Depression among Women—a Prospective
Cohort Study," *Annals of Behavioral Medicine* 50,
no. 6 (December 2016): 876–84, https://academic
.oup.com/abm/article/50/6/876/4562664.

  Full Gospel Businessmen's Training, "47 Health
Benefits of Prayer," https://fgbt.org/Health-Tips
/47-health-benefits-of-prayer.html.

81. Christina M. Karns, William E. Moore III, and
Ulrich Mayr, "The Cultivation of Pure Altruism
via Gratitude: A Functional MRI Study of Change
with Gratitude Practice," *Frontiers in Human
Neuroscience* 11 (December 2017): article 599,
https://doi.org/10.3389/fnhum.2017.00599.

82. Michael Wines, "In Memoir, Barbara Bush Recalls
Private Trials of a Political Life," *New York Times*,
September 8, 1994, http://www.nytimes.com

/1994/09/08/us/in-memoir-barbara-bush-recalls
-private-trials-of-a-political-life.html.

"Barbara Bush Says She Fought Depression in
'76," *Washington Post*, May 20, 1990, https://www
.washingtonpost.com/archive/politics/1990/05/20
/barbara-bush-says-she-fought-depression-in-76
/0ac40655-923e-448d-bfcc-aa3ea5cb88c8/?utm
_term=.1bb20fdb6707.

83. K. E. Buchanan and A. Bardi, "Acts of Kindness
and Acts of Novelty Affect Life Satisfaction,"
Journal of Social Psychology 150, no. 3 (May–June
2010): 235–37, https://doi.org/10.1080
/00224540903365554.

84. L. B. Aknin et al., "Happiness Runs in a Circular
Motion: Evidence for a Positive Feedback Loop
between Prosocial Spending and Happiness," *Journal
of Happiness Studies* 13, no. 2 (April 2012): 347–55,
https://doi.org/10.1007/s10902-011-9267-5.

85. S. Q. Park et al., "A Neural Link between Generosity
and Happiness," *Nature Communications* 8 (2017):
15964, https://doi.org/10.1038/ncomms15964;
S. G. Post, "Altruism, Happiness, and Health:
It's Good to Be Good," *International Journal of
Behavioral Medicine* 12, no. 2 (2005): 66–77,
https://doi.org/10.1207/s15327558ijbm1202_4.

L. B. Aknin, J. Kiley Hamlin, and Elizabeth W.
Dunn, "Giving Leads to Happiness in Young
Children," *PLOS One* 7, no. 6 (2012): e39211,
https://doi.org/10.1371/journal.pone.0039211.